D1316691

AUBURN

MORE DAILY DEVOTIONS FOR DIE-HARD FANS

TIGERS

MORE AUBURN

More Daily Devotions for Die-Hard Fans: Auburn Tigers
© 2013 Ed McMinn
Extra Point Publishers; P.O. Box 871; Perry, GA 31069

Library of Congress Cataloging-in-Publication Data
13 ISBN Digit ISBN: 978-0-9882595-8-4

Manufactured in the United States of America.

Visit us at www.die-hardfans.com.

Cover and interior design by Slynn McMinn.

Every effort has been made to identify copyright holders. Any
omissions are unintentional. Extra Point Publishers should be notified
in writing immediately for full acknowledgement in future editions.

TIGERS

A Note from the Author

This is actually Volume II of *Daily Devotions for Die-Hard Fans: Auburn Tigers*. The devotions and their stories are all new, written for this book. Many, but not all, of the devotions center on the 2010 football national championship.

As with the first volume (which is still available), my hope is that you enjoy this humble offering. My prayer is that it in some way proves beneficial to you in your faith life.

-- Ed McMinn

The following titles are available:

DAY 1

A HELPING HAND

Read Psalm 121.

"My help comes from the Lord, the maker of heaven and earth" (v. 2).

The offense needed some help; the defense was more than glad to lend a hand.

The Auburn offense of 2010 finished seventh in the nation by gaining a whopping 499.2 yards a game. In the last half, though, of the SEC opener against Mississippi State on Sept. 9, the offense had trouble getting out of its own way.

The Tigers rung up 52 points on Arkansas State in the 2010 opener, and the offense looked unstoppable again on its opening possession the following Thursday. Sophomore receiver Emory Blake caught a 39-yard TD pass from Cam Newton only 3:46 into the game. In the second quarter, Newton hit junior wide receiver Darvin Adams with a 12-yard TD pass, and Wes Byrum booted a 34-yard field goal for a 17-7 halftime lead.

That was it, however. The offense put no points on the board in the last half and finished with 349 yards, only a few dozen more than the infamous 3-2 win over MSU two seasons before. State opened the last half with a flawless 13-play drive that made it 17-14; after that, the Auburn defense had to step up.

State blocked a field goal and got the ball with 2:19 left needing only a field goal to tie. The Auburn offense "could do nothing but stand on the sideline and yell as their defensive counterparts went to work." A pass interference call moved the Bulldogs into Auburn territory. But then All-American tackle Nick Fairley and linebacker Josh Bynes pressured MSU's quarterback, and cornerback T'Sharvan Bell and safety Zac Etheridge smothered the Dog receivers. State threw four straight incomplete passes, and the sideline exploded with joy.

In the locker room, the winners locked arms and sang "Lean on Me" – which is exactly what they had done in helping each other out and taking a tough win.

As do the Tigers in a tightly contested game, we have our ups and downs. Sometimes – often more than once in the journey that is our life – we get to a point when our own resources won't get us through. We need help.

But where to turn? Family and friends? Counselors? Even a pastor? They're certainly better options than the likes of drugs or alcohol. But they're fallible people, and the truth is they sometimes let us down. They simply, for whatever reason, can't or won't provide what we need.

They're derivative anyway; that is, they were all created. The answer for meaningful, life-changing help that will never fail is the Source – Almighty God. God cares for his people, each one of us. The creator of the cosmos cares about you. He knows you by name and knows exactly what's going on in your life. And he has the power and the desire to help – as no one or nothing else can.

That's what we've got to do all year. We've got to lean on each other.
-- Nick Fairley after the MSU game

"May I help you?" isn't just for a store; it's
a question God will ask if you turn to him.

DAY 2

HOMEWORK

Read Joshua 1:1-9.

"Do not let this Book of the Law depart from your mouth; meditate on it day and night, so that you may be careful to do everything written in it. Then you will be prosperous and successful" (v. 8).

Auburn's 2010 national championship may well have been won by some players who went mental rather than physical.

The Oregon Ducks headed into the BCS title game of Jan. 10, 2011, described as "the best offense around," a flashy sideshow in wacky and garish uniform combinations. Lined up against them was the Auburn defense, of whom it was said they had given up "more real estate than Donald Trump owns." They had, after all, surrendered 20-or-more points nine times.

But defensive coordinator Ted Roof defended his defenders. "The thing about this group is when they're challenged they've responded," he said. Oregon certainly challenged them, but they were ready in large part because they did their homework.

The preparation that was key to the game for the defense took place to a large extent in the film room. For weeks on end, the defenders watched films of that much-ballyhood offense. They just did it differently: They kept watching it faster and faster and faster. As a result, said linebacker Craig Stevens, when the defenders saw the real thing in the game, Oregon was "going a little slower, and [we were able] to recognize things."

Just had good was the Auburn defense that glorious night? They held Oregon to its second-lowest point total of the season (19) and the nation's leading rusher to just 49 yards. They intercepted the Duck quarterback twice. They so dominated the red zone that "Oregon's futility near the goal line will be [the Duck head coach's] most frustrating memories" of the game.

"I feel like we earned a lot of respect tonight," Stevens said about the defense after the game. That and a national title.

One of the most enduring illusions of adolescence is that once you graduate from high school and/or college, the homework ends. Life requires constant, ongoing study, however. In many ways, you assemble a life, much as you would a bicycle for your children. You know the drill; even with parts scattered all over the garage, you work undismayed because you can read the instructions and follow them. With the bicycle assembled and ready to race the wind, you nod in satisfaction. Mission completed.

Wouldn't it be great if life, too, had an instruction book, a set of directions that can lead you to a productive, rewarding life so that as its end you can nod in satisfaction and declare "Mission completed"?

It does. Life's instruction book is probably by your bed or on a living room table. It's the Bible, given to you by God to guide you through life. But for it to do you any good, you must read it; you must do your homework.

Our defense did its homework and did the job.
-- Cam Newton after the win over Oregon

**The Bible is God's instruction book with
directions on how to assemble your life.**

DAY 3

LONELY TIMES

Read 1 Kings 19:1-10.

"I alone am left, and they are seeking my life, to take it away" (v. 10b).

Standing by yourself on a platform 33 feet above a pool of water seems like a really lonely place to be in. But Caesar Garcia was never alone up there.

Garcia is one of the greatest divers in Auburn and collegiate history. In both 2003 and 2004, he won the NCAA platform diving national championship, the only person in history to win back-to-back titles. He also won the SEC titles both seasons, was the NCAA Diver of the Year in 2004, and earned a spot on the 2004 U.S. Olympic Team. He won the SEC's H. Boyd McWhorter Award in 2004 as the league's top male athlete.

Certainly Garcia had to climb that platform and stand alone with everyone watching him as he prepared to dive. He also appreciated the dangers involved in his sport. But he never felt alone and he always felt he had some help – because of his faith. "If you're jumping off of a 33-foot platform doing multiple flips and twists, faith helps," Garcia said. "I like to imagine (God) spotting me just in case something goes wrong."

Keenly aware that God was with him, Garcia prayed frequently during competitions. He asked that God help him "keep my head on straight. . . . What I ask for is to be happy with my performance and to be gracious regardless of the outcome."

TIGERS

His faith was always a big part of Garcia's diving career. He was an altar server throughout high school in Baton Rouge. Before he left for Athens and the Olympics in 2004, an uncle reminded him to "Give God the glory in everything you do."

Garcia faithfully tried to do just that. After all, God climbed with him up that platform.

We all know loneliness even – strangely enough -- sometimes when we're standing in the midst of a crowd. Like love, fear, and despair, loneliness is an elemental part of "the human condition"; it's universal.

Every single one of us is alone in a sense because we can never completely bridge the gap between our consciousness and that of another person, even the ones we love best. We can't really know another person; that person can't really know us. We are all strangers to each other.

There is one powerful exception, however: Almighty God. As Elijah found out and as Caesar Garcia knew, God is always with us, knowing exactly what we are experiencing, thinking, and feeling. God meets us in the deepest and darkest corners of our hearts and minds. Through the Holy Spirit, God is not just with us as other people are but is in us as other people can never be.

The heartwarming truth is that the person of faith is not alone and never will be. God is with us always, even when we don't notice.

I never pray about winning, but I thank God when it happens.
-- Caesar Garcia on God's presence during his competitions

**Loneliness is part of being human – until we
know God, and then we're never alone again.**

DAY 4

RUN FOR IT

Read John 20:1-10.

*"Peter and the other disciple started for the tomb. Both
were running, but the other disciple outran Peter and
reached the tomb first" (vv. 3-4).*

In an epic battle of unbeaten Tigers, Auburn's 2010 season was
up for grabs -- until Onterio McCalebb went for a run.

On Oct. 23, Auburn hosted undefeated and sixth-ranked LSU
in a game that would destroy the national and SEC title hopes of
one team of cats. On the field, Auburn blew LSU out of Jordan-
Hare. The Tigers set a school record against an SEC opponent by
rushing for 440 yards. For the game, Auburn would outgain LSU
by almost three hundred yards of total offense.

Yet, as the game wore on, the scoreboard told a different story,
one that was closer to the truth: The game was a real dogfight
in which everything didn't go Auburn's way. "There were a lot
of times in that game that it did not look good," said head coach
Gene Chizik after the game.

The Tigers used a 1-yard run from Cam Newton and a 42-yard
field goal from Wes Byrum to lead 10-3 in the second quarter.
Despite all that offense, though, the Tigers scored only once on
their next seven possessions. That was on a 49-yard romp by
Newton in the third quarter that put Auburn up 17-10.

The offensively-challenged Tigers from Baton Rouge got 39 of
their game total of 128 passing yards on one fourth-quarter play

that tied the game at 17. After an exchange of punts, the Auburn offense set up shop at its own 10 with 6:10 to play.

Newton broke for 16 yards before freshman tailback Michael Dyer added four more. That's when McCalebb shook the venerable stadium to its foundations. He took a handoff, hit his left tackle, made one cut, and suddenly found himself running in the open field. He didn't slow down until he had run 70 yards, all the way to glory and the LSU end zone.

24-17. Auburn was running straight toward the national title.

Hit the ground running -- every morning that's what you do as you leave the house and re-enter the rat race. You run errands; you run though a presentation; you give someone a run for his money; you always want to be in the running and never run-of-the-mill.

You're always running toward something, such as your goals, or away from something, such as your past. Many of us spend much of our lives foolhardily trying to run away from God, the purposes he has for us, and the blessings he is waiting to give us.

No matter how hard or how far you run, though, you can never outrun yourself or God. God keeps pace with you, calling you in the short run to take care of the long run by falling to your knees and running for your life -- to Jesus -- just as Peter and the other disciple ran that first Easter morning.

On your knees, you run all the way to glory.

You feel good when they tell you you ran for 440 yards against the No. 3 defense in the country.

-- *Auburn center Ryan Pugh*

You can run to eternity by going to your knees.

DAY 5

BELIEVE IT

Read John 3:16-21.

"For God so loved the world that He gave His only begotten Son, that whoever believes in Him should not perish but have everlasting life" (v. 16 NKJV).

It took a last-half comeback for the 1957 Auburn Tigers to believe they could win the national championship.

The season got off to a big start with a 7-0 win over the 8th-ranked Tennessee Volunteers in Knoxville. That earned Auburn a spot in the top 10, and the Tigers kept moving up as they kept winning. They were 6-0 after beating 19th-ranked Florida 13-0. That set up a big game against 17th-ranked Mississippi State.

A 1958 All-American at center, Jackie Burkett recalled that the Tigers trailed 7-0 at halftime (the only time all season Auburn fell behind) and that head coach Shug Jordan had a lot to say to them in the locker room. "Shug made a good speech in there," Burkett remembered. He told his players they were better than State and reminded them of their record and their national ranking. "It was like, 'Hey, we have a lot on the line here,'" Burkett said.

The Tigers came out roaring the last half and didn't stop. They took the opening kickoff and ground out a touchdown. Fullback Billy Atkins, who set a school scoring record that season with 81 points, got the six points.

After the kickoff, the defense that led the nation in rushing yards and total yards forced a Bulldog punt. What resulted was

TIGERS

one of the biggest plays of the season.

Burkett tore through the Bulldog line and jumped up so high that he was "way up over the punter." The desperate kicker pulled the ball down, tried to run, and was tackled by end John Whatley for a safety. The Tigers would not surrender the lead; another Atkins score made it a 15-7 final.

Burkett said, "I believe that game was the turning point of our national championship season." That's because with the tough win, the Tigers really believed they could win every game.

What we believe underscores everything about our lives. Our politics. How we raise our children. How we treat other people. Whether we respect others, their property, and their lives.

Often, competing belief systems clamor for our attention; we all know persons – maybe friends and family members – who have lost Christianity in the shuffle and the hubbub. We turn aside from believing in Christ at our peril, however, because the heart and soul, the very essence of Christianity, is belief. That is, believing that Jesus is the very Son of God and that it is through him – and only through him – that we can find forgiveness and salvation that will reserve a place for us with God.

But believing is more than simply acknowledging intellectually that Jesus is God. Even the demons who serve Satan know that. It is belief so deep that we entrust our lives and our eternity to Christ. We live like we believe it – because we do.

After [the State win] we said, 'By golly, we can win every game.'
-- Jackie Burkett

Believe it: Jesus is the way – and the only way –
to eternal life with God.

DAY 6

GOOD LUCK

Read Acts 1:15-25.

*"Then they prayed, 'Lord, you know everyone's heart.
Show us which of these two you have chosen.' . . . Then
they cast lots" (vv. 24, 25a).*

The Luck Stops Here." Yes, it did. Auburn didn't need a bit of luck to break the Florida Gators' hearts.

That sign about luck coming to a screeching halt fluttered from a Gator section in The Swamp on the afternoon of Oct. 15, 1994. It was a swipe at the Tigers and their 17-game win streak, the product the sign asserted of luck, not talent.

The Tigers had certainly won their share of games theatrically during the streak, the nation's longest, and many pundits and critics called it luck. That was largely because Auburn had come from behind ten times in the fourth quarter during the streak. But as *Sports Illustrated*'s Sally Jenkins put it, "That is not a matter of good fortune; that is a matter of talent, fervent belief in themselves, and inspired coaching."

Nevertheless, the 6th-ranked Tigers went into the game against the top-ranked Gators a ridiculous 17-point underdog. The two powerhouses battled all afternoon with Florida taking a 33-29 lead with 5:51 left to play. With little more than a minute in the game, the Tigers took over at their own 45 after an interception by safety Brian Robinson when Florida for some reason threw the ball rather than waiting to punt Auburn into a deep hole.

TIGERS

Quarterback Patrick Nix quickly led his team down the field. With 30 seconds on the clock, from the Florida 8, Nix spotted single coverage on 6-2 wideout Frank Sanders and lofted the ball to him. He easily outjumped a shorter defender for a touchdown that was anything but lucky. Auburn won 36-33

"As for luck," Jenkins wrote, "the only thing that stopped was the suggestion that Auburn couldn't win without it."

Ever think sometimes that other people have all the luck? Some guy wins a lottery while you can't get a raise of a few lousy bucks at work. The football takes a lucky bounce the other team's way and Auburn loses a game. If you have any luck to speak of, it's bad.

To ascribe anything that happens in life to blind luck, however, is to believe that random chance controls everything, including you. But here's the truth: There is no such thing as luck, good or bad. Even when the apostles in effect flipped a coin to pick the new guy, they acknowledged that the lots merely revealed to them a decision God had already made.

It's true that we can't explain why some people skate merrily through life while others suffer in horrifying ways. We don't know why good things happen to bad people and vice versa. But none of it results from luck, unless you want to attribute that name to the force that does indeed control the universe; you know -- the one more commonly called God.

This wasn't a fluke. You can't call this luck.
-- Patrick Nix on the '94 win over Florida

**A force does exist that is in charge,
but it isn't luck; it's God.**

GOOD NEWS

Read Matthew 28:1-10.

'"He has risen from the dead and is going ahead of you into Galilee. There you will see him.' Now I have told you" (v. 7).

The news spread quickly: Auburn was Number One.

After the fourth-ranked Tigers defeated sixth-ranked LSU 24-17 on Oct. 23, 2010, they jumped to the top of the BCS rankings for the first time in history. Like the proverbial wildfire, the word raced across campus and through the dorms. "Everybody's tweeting about it right now," said senior safety Zac Etheridge, forced to mute his ringer to talk. His phone started ringing within seconds of the poll's publication, one ring after another as reporters called for interviews and friends and teammates called to share in the excitement. "It means a lot," confessed linebacker Craig Stevens.

The lofty ranking came with warnings, however, from Gene Chizik and his coaches. They regarded the news as a major distraction from the real purpose: winning the next football game (against Ole Miss). "We just had a team meeting," the head Tiger said, "and we talked about being very grounded and understanding that every week is another new week."

In this case, though, the number-one ranking was as dangerous as a minefield. For three straight weeks, the team ranked No. 1 had lost: Alabama to South Carolina, Ohio State to Wisconsin, and Oklahoma to Missouri. With 3-4 Ole Miss dead ahead, left guard Mike Berry was cautious. "You don't take [any]one lightly," he said. "Everybody's trying to win."

By Saturday, the ranking was old news. The Tigers whipped the Rebels 51-31 – and inexplicably dropped to No. 2 behind Oregon. As it turned out, the really big news was not that Auburn was ranked No. 1 in October but that the Tigers were ranked No. 1 when the season ended.

The story of mankind's "progress" through the millennia could be summarized and illustrated quite well in an account of how we disseminate our news. For much of recorded history, we told our stories through word of mouth, which required time to spread across political and geographical boundaries. That method also didn't do much to ensure accuracy.

Today, though, our news – like Auburn's being ranked No. 1 -- is instantaneous. Yesterday's news is old news; we want to see it and hear about it as it happens.

But the biggest news story in the history of the world goes virtually unnoticed every day by the so-called mainstream media. It is, in fact, often treated as nothing more than superstition. But it's true, and it is the greatest, most wonderful news of all.

What headline should be blaring from every news source in the world? This one: "Jesus Rises from Dead, Defeats Death." It's still today's news, and it's still the most important news story ever.

As a team, we don't even think about it. That's something to get our fans excited.
-- Zac Etheridge on hearing the news that Auburn was ranked No. 1

The biggest news story in history took place when Jesus Christ walked out of that tomb.

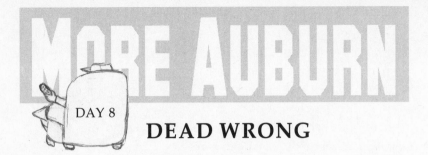

DAY 8

DEAD WRONG

Read Matthew 26:14-16; 27:1-10.

"When Judas, who had betrayed him, saw that Jesus was condemned, he was seized with remorse" (v. 27:3).

Auburn fans will forever give thanks that the Alabama coaching staff was wrong about Bo Jackson.

The man generally recognized as the greatest athlete in school history and one of the most iconic figures in all of college football arrived on the Plains in 1982. He had chosen to make only one official recruiting visit, and that was to Auburn.

Second-year head coach Pat Dye and assistant Bobby Wallace bluntly told Jackson their situation at running back was dire, so they were recruiting a whole batch of backs. Dye told him, "If you work hard, if you do what you are supposed to, I will give you every chance in the book to be a starter." Dye meant right away.

The only other school Jackson considered was Alabama "I was an Alabama fan, and I wanted to go there," he said. The coaches told him he would probably not play until the end of his sophomore year or the start of his junior year. But there was more to Jackson's recruitment than that, though he never did figure it out.

Alabama's defensive coordinator was assigned to recruit him. Only more than two decades later did Jackson learn from his high school coach what that meant. Playing golf with his coach one day, Jackson asked him why Alabama sent the defensive coordinator to recruit him. The coach just laughed at him and said, "You don't know?" Alabama was recruiting him to be a linebacker!

That same Alabama coach who told Jackson he wouldn't play right away also told him that if he went to Auburn, he would never beat the Tide. After Jackson went over the top for the game-winning touchdown in the 23-22 win over Alabama in '82, he made eye contact with his Alabama recruiter and gave him a look that said very clearly, "You were wrong."

He was really wrong. Auburn came right back to make it two in a row over Alabama in '83.

There's wrong, there's dead wrong, and there's Judas wrong. We've all been wrong in our lives, but we can at least honestly ease our conscience by telling ourselves we'll never be as wrong as Judas was. A close examination of Judas' actions, however, reveals that we can indeed replicate in our own lives the mistake Judas made that drove him to suicidal despair.

Judas ultimately regretted his betrayal of our Lord, but his sorrow and remorse, however boundless, could not save him. His attempt to undo his initial wrong was futile because he tried to fix everything himself rather than turning to God in repentance and begging for mercy.

While we can't literally betray Jesus to his enemies as Judas did, we can match Judas' failure in our own lives by not turning to God in Jesus' name and asking for forgiveness for our sins. In that case, we ultimately will be as dead wrong as Judas was.

There's nothing wrong with the car except that it's on fire.
-- Formula One racing commentator Murray Walker

A sin is the first wrong; failing to ask God
for forgiveness of it is the second.

DAY 9

THE LAST WORD

Read Luke 9:22-27.

*"The Son of Man . . . must be killed and on the third day
be raised to life. . . . [S]ome who are standing here will . . .
see the kingdom of God" (vv. 22, 27).*

In a game that set an SEC record for points scored, it was the
Auburn defense, strangely enough, that had the last word.

The seventh-ranked Tigers were 6-0 when they hosted the 4-1,
12th-ranked Arkansas Razorbacks on Oct. 16, 2010. The pundits
and the fans expected a shootout; what they got was a nuclear ex-
plosion. The two teams combined for 108 points, breaking the old
conference record of 104 points for a non-overtime game.

"Injured, exhausted and exposed, the Auburn defense looked
overmatched [in] giving up 43 points and 566 yards." When the
game was on the line in the fourth quarter, though, that bunch
that Arkansas spent most of the day manhandling rose up to be
the difference in the outcome.

The two offensive powerhouses matched each other point for
point through the first three quarters and on into the final period.
Both defenses "oscillated between non-existent and passable."
The Tigers, in fact, would eventually score their most points ever
in an SEC game, 65. But when Arkansas scored one minute into
the fourth quarter, the Hogs led 43-37. To no one's surprise, Auburn answered with a 68-yard TD drive, the score coming on a
15-yard pass from Cam Newton to wide receiver Emory Blake.

TIGERS

That's when something unexpected happened: The Auburn defense showed up. Linebacker Craig Stevens and tackle Mike Blanc forced a fumble that safety Zac Etheridge scooped up and took 47 yards for the first defensive touchdown of the year. Linebacker Josh Bynes then grabbed interceptions on Arkansas' next two possessions. They set up a pair of touchdown runs.

The final score was a mind-boggling, record-setting 65-43 -- and the buzz after the game was about the Auburn defense.

Why is it that -- unlike the Auburn defense, which had its say in the nick of time against Arkansas -- we often come up with the last word -- the perfect zinger -- only long after the incident that called for a smart and pithy rejoinder is over? "Man, I shoulda said that! That woulda fixed his wagon!" But it's too late.

Nobody in history, though, including us, could ever hope to match the man who had the greatest last word of them all: Jesus Christ. His enemies killed him and put him in a tomb, confident they were done with that nuisance for good. Instead, they were unwitting participants in God's great plan of redemption and gave the last word to Jesus. He has it still.

Jesus didn't go to that cross so he could die; he went to that cross so all those who follow him might live. Because of Jesus' own death on the cross, the final word for us is not our own death. Rather it is life, through our salvation in Jesus Christ.

Once we got that fumble, that just turned the momentum over and strengthened our defense, gave us a little bit of confidence out there.
-- Linebacker Craig Stevens on the defense's late surge vs. Arkansas

With Jesus, the last word is always life
and is never death.

DAY 10

UNCERTAIN TIMES

Read Psalm 18:1-6, 20-29.

"The Lord is my rock . . . in whom I take refuge. He is my shield, and the horn of my salvation, my stronghold" (v. 2).

When the Tigers of 2010 gathered in the fall, about the only certain thing anyone could say about the team was that it was less uncertain than recent Auburn teams had been.

In 2009, Gene Chizik's first year on the Plains as the head coach, the Tigers went 8-5. Expectations were reasonably low for that season, but when 2010 rolled around, many Tiger fans and the pundits in general didn't know what to do with their expectations. One thing was certain: Nobody was seriously and earnestly talking national championship. "It should be the goal," said senior linebacker Josh Bynes. "The expectations are there now." He was speaking of making it to the league championship game in Atlanta. About the only certain declaration a pundit would make was Evan Woodbery's "the promise for this season is real."

Much of the promise lay in the certainty that for the first time in a while did underlie the program. For one thing, the players had their entire coaching staff back. Every single assistant coach joined Chizik for a second season. "There are guys on our football team right now who for the first time in their career have the same coordinator for the second year in a row," Chizik said. "I [think] that [is] extremely important."

TIGERS

Another certainty was that the Tiger defense in 2010 would have more depth. As linebacker Craig Stevens put it, the days of "having to go out there and run 100 plays non-stop" were over. That depth was the product of a deep and talented senior class and two solid recruiting classes, including a top-five bunch.

Certainly, Auburn would have a good season in 2010. Just how good remained uncertain – then.

Even when we believe the Tigers will field a good team we have some uncertainty because football just isn't a sure thing. If it were, it wouldn't be any fun.

But life itself is much like an SEC game between two top-ten teams. We never know what's in store for us or what's going to happen next. We can be riding high one day with a job promotion, good health, a nice family, and sunny weather. Only a short time later, we can be unemployed, sick, divorced, and/or broke.

When we place our trust in life itself and its rewards, we are certain to face uncertain times.

We must search out a haven, a place where we know we can find shelter when life's storms buffet us and knock us down. Right there on our knees, we can find that rock. Right there on our knees, we can find that certainty – every time.

Our life and times are uncertain. The Lord God Almighty is sure – and is only a prayer away.

Any time you have the same coaching staff, there's a confidence there.
-- Tackle Lee Ziemba on the effect of the coaches' return

The world and everything and everybody in it are uncertain; only God offers certainty in our lives no matter what happens.

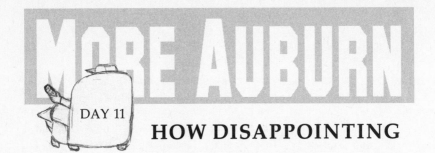

HOW DISAPPOINTING

Read Ezra 3.

*"Many of the older priests and Levites and family heads,
who had seen the former temple, wept aloud when they
saw the foundation of this temple being laid, while many
others shouted for joy" (v. 12).*

One of college football's cherished adages is that seasons are really won from January to July. If that old saw were true, then Auburn was headed for a disappointing season in 2004.

Coaches insist that the time when players are "lifting, running, stretching and building themselves into better football players" is the time when championship seasons are made. In 2004, everything head strength and conditioning coach Kevin Yoxall saw during that time convinced him the Tigers were headed for a long season.

"I've had other winter and spring training periods where it went better," Yoxall admitted. "We didn't have a lot of colossal numbers in our testing."

The numbers weren't all that was disappointing, though; the players' attitudes about the workouts left Yoxall fretting.

Since NCAA rules prohibited teams from holding mandatory workouts from Jan. 1 to May 31, Yoxall resorted to "discretionary" weeks in which players were encouraged, but not required, to report for daily workouts. Yoxall expected a strong turnout after the end of spring football.

TIGERS

So he met with the players before finals and told them what he expected of them in the way of the "voluntary" workouts, but the response was disappointing. "Let's be honest," he said. "Most of these kids are 18 to 21 years old, and I didn't have a lot of them show up. I was really kind of disappointed."

As history shows, though, nothing about the Tigers' performance on the field was disappointing that season as they went undefeated and were SEC champions.

We know disappointment. Friends lie to us or betray us; we lose our jobs through no fault of our own; emotional distance grows between us and our children; the Tigers lose; our dreams shatter.

Disappointment occurs when something or somebody fails to meet our expectations, which inevitably will happen. What is crucial to our life, therefore, is not avoiding disappointment but handling it.

One alternative is to act as the old people of Israel did at the dedication of the temple. Instead of joyously celebrating the construction of a new place of worship, they wailed and moaned about the lost glories of the old one. They chose disappointment over lost glories rather than the wonders of the present reality.

Disappointment can paralyze us all, but only if we lose sight of an immutable truth: Our lives may not always be what we wish they were, but God is still good to us.

There's nothing disappointing about that.

I was very concerned because we were behind where we needed to be.
-- Kevin Yoxall on the disappointing spring workouts

Even in disappointing times, we can be confident that God is with us and therefore life is good.

DAY 12

THE GOOD FIGHT

Read 2 Corinthians 10:1-6.

"Though we live in the world, we do not wage war as the world does. The weapons we fight with are not the weapons of the world" (vv. 3-4a).

Auburn nose guard Benji Roland once got into a fight with a coach at practice -- and was praised for it.

Roland was a three-year starter (1986-88) for squads that went 29-5-2, won two SEC championships, and whipped the Tide three straight times. He was All-America in 1988 and was the leader on a defense that led the nation in total defense, rushing defense, and scoring defense.

Roland was a tough, feisty player who didn't mind at all getting into a scrap or two if he felt the situation warranted it, even if that included an assistant coach.

Wayne Hall was the defensive line coach and the defensive co-ordinator at the time. Roland remembered him as "an ornery old guy" who "demanded and expected perfection." He was also "a moody guy" who "would always grab you and put his hands on you." Roland recalled that head coach Pat Dye's rule was that if a coach put his hands on a player, he was on his own.

One practice, Hall was hollering at Roland, who didn't take too kindly to it, and the two "tied up with one another." The tussle escalated when Hall ripped Roland's helmet off. Finally, tackle Stacy Searels grabbed Roland, and offensive line coach Neil Callaway latched onto Hall and separated them.

After practice, Roland looked up the coach for a final word. He told Hall, "Coach, you put your hands on me. I'm a grown man. I am going to fight you back if you put your hands on me."

The next day as Roland was walking to practice, Dye surprised him by telling him, "I was pulling for you yesterday." Roland said, "Sir?" "Yeah," the head Tiger said. "If I got a player who can't whip my coaches, you're not gonna play for me."

Violence is not the Christian way, but what about confrontation? Following Jesus' admonition to turn the other cheek has rendered many a Christian meek and mild in the name of obedience. But we need to remember that the Lord we follow once bullwhipped a bunch of folks who turned God's temple into a flea market.

With Christianity in America under attack as never before, we must stand up for and fight for our faith. Who else is there to stand up for Jesus if not you? Our pretty little planet -- including our nation -- is a battleground between good and evil. We are far from helpless in this fight because God has provided us with a powerful set of weapons. Prayer, faith, hope, love, the Word of God itself and the Holy Spirit -- these are the weapons at our command with which to vanquish evil and godlessness.

We are called by God to use them, to fight the good fight, not just in our own lives but in our nation and in our world.

I wasn't taking his stuff that day.
-- Benji Roland on his fight with Wayne Hall

**'Stand Up, Stand Up for Jesus' is not
an antiquated hymn but is a contemporary call
to battle for our Lord.**

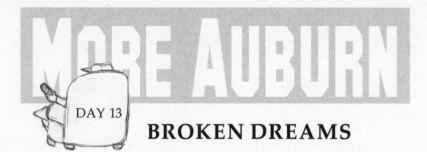

BROKEN DREAMS

Read Joel 2:28-32.

"I will pour out my Spirit on all people. . . . Your old men will dream dreams" (v. 28).

Kodi Burns gave up on his dream. Auburn was a better football team for it.

Burns was a four-star quarterback recruit out of Fort Smith, Ark. In his freshman and sophomore seasons of 2007 and 2008, his lifelong dream of playing quarterback seemed to be coming true. In 2008, he started seven games under center for the Tigers.

Before the 2009 season, however, Burns "made the most difficult decision of his life": He gave up on his dream of playing quarterback. At a meeting in August, he told his teammates he had asked the coaches for a chance to play wide receiver.

Burns was led to surrender his dream by his sense that Chris Todd was a better fit for the team at quarterback. He couldn't know it at the time, of course, but he certainly wouldn't have seen any action at quarterback in 2010.

It wasn't that Burns knew anything about his new position. "I'd never caught a pass in my life," he said. With such a short time before the 2009 season began, "They kinda threw me out there." The coaches admitted as much. "He was a quarterback playing wide receiver" in 2009, said offensive coordinator Gus Malzahn.

Nevertheless, Burns had a productive year. He ran for five touchdowns and threw for two more in the wildcat formation installed to take advantage of his talents. He caught five passes for 46 yards, including a touchdown against Georgia.

With a season and a spring practice behind him, Burns became an excellent blocker in 2010. He hauled in 11 passes, including a 35-yard touchdown catch in the national championship game.

Burns was so respected by his teammates for his selflessness and his attitude that they selected him to present a team jersey and helmet to the president when the BCS champions visited the White House.

For Kodi Burns, realized dreams replaced broken ones.

We all have particular dreams. Perhaps to make a million dollars, write the Great American Novel, go into business for ourselves, or play quarterback. More likely than not, however, we gradually lose our hold on those dreams. They slip away from us as we surrender them to the reality of everyday living.

But we also have general dreams. For world peace. For an end to hunger. That no child should ever again be afraid. These dreams we hold doggedly onto as if something inside us tells us that even though the world gets itself into a bigger mess every year, one day everything will be all right.

That's because it will be. God has promised a time when his spirit will rule the world. Jesus spoke of a time when he will return to claim his kingdom. In that day, our dreams of peace and plenty and the banishment of hate and want will be reality.

Our dreams based on God's promises will come true.

We wouldn't be the team we are today without Kodi setting the example.
-- Guard Mike Berry in 2010

Dreams based on God's promises will come true.

DAY 14

THE HEALING TOUCH

Read Matthew 17:14-20.

"If you have faith as small as a mustard seed, you can say to this mountain, 'Move from here to there' and it will move. Nothing will be impossible for you" (v. 20).

The doctors said Steve Gandy would miss the entire 2006 season, but they didn't have the linebacker's faith in God's healing power.

During two-a-days prior to the season, Gandy, a sophomore, suffered a deep thigh bruise from a hard hit. He iced it down, but later that evening his thigh swelled to the point that he was honestly afraid his leg would burst. He called a trainer, who called a team physician, who called Gandy and told him to get to an emergency room immediately.

The doctor had cause to be concerned. The blow to Gandy's thigh had caused swelling to an extent that collapse of the blood vessels was a possibility, leading to loss of the leg or death. Gandy underwent emergency surgery to allow the fluid to drain. The incision from his hip to his knee required one hundred stitches to repair. As Gandy recovered in the hospital, the doctors told him that he would not be able to play at all in 2006. Gandy didn't buy it.

Instead, when he was released, he went to work with strength coach Kevin Yoxall. He also asked his teammates at the team's Friday night prayer meeting to pray for healing.

Team chaplain Chette Williams said Gandy became "an inspiration to the guys on the field with his hard work and his own prayers." Nevertheless, when Auburn opened the season against Washington State, he was on the sideline in his street clothes.

Three weeks later, though, at the Friday night prayer meeting, Gandy offered up a prayer of thanksgiving and praise for God's healing touch. This young man of faith whom doctors had said would miss the whole season started the next day against Buffalo. He played in every game the rest of the season.

If we believe in miraculous healing at all, we have pretty much come to consider it to be a relatively rare occurrence. All too often, when we are ill or hurting we rely totally on doctors and pills without even thinking of asking God to heal us. We just don't share Steve Gandy's abiding faith. If we really want to move a mountain, we'll round up some heavy-duty earthmoving equipment.

The truth is, though, that divine healing occurs with quite astonishing regularity; the problem is our perspective. We are usually quite effusive in our thanks to and praise for a doctor or a particular medicine without considering that God is the one who is responsible for all healing.

We should remember also that "natural" healing occurs because our bodies react as God created them to. Those healings, too, are divine; they, too, are miraculous. Faith healing is really nothing more – or less – than giving credit where credit is due.

Whenever you've gone through anything as dramatic as he went through, you need to protect him.
-- Tommy Tuberville on resting Steve Gandy some in his first game back

God does in fact heal continuously everywhere;
all too often we just don't notice.

DAY 15

NEVER TOO LATE

Read John 11:17-27, 38-44.

"'But, Lord," said Martha, . . . "he has been there four days.' Then Jesus said, 'Did I not tell you that if you believed, you would see the glory of God?'" (vv. 19b-40)

For Travis Williams, a slot berth in the national title game came late, but at least it came.

With the 21-13 win over Alabama on Nov. 20, 2004, the Tigers finished the regular season 11-0 but were ranked third behind USC and Oklahoma. Unless one of those two teams lost, Auburn would probably be left out of the national title game no matter how badly they trounced Tennessee in the SEC championship game.

That's exactly the way it turned out. Auburn beat the Vols 38-28 but wound up in New Orleans in the Sugar Bowl as a consolation prize "We're honored to be in the Sugar Bowl," said quarterback Jason Campbell, "but in our hearts we still feel like we should be playing for the championship."

One of those disappointed Tigers that season was junior linebacker Travis Williams. He was a three-year starter who was First-Team All-SEC in 2004 and second-team in 2005. After a brief stint with the Falcons, Williams joined Gene Chizik's first coaching staff in 2009 as a graduate assistant.

As the 2010 season unfolded, Williams found himself in an unusual position. If Auburn could win the SEC, he would be the only member of that 2004 team to get another shot at the title. Many of

TIGERS

his former teammates knew it, too. A number of them regularly called him to make sure the guys of 2010 understood that they had a once-in-a lifetime chance that the 2004 team hadn't had.

Williams didn't let the 2010 Tigers forget, but with the 56-17 romp over the Gamecocks for the SEC title, he didn't have to worry anymore. Six years after he should have been going, Williams was headed for the title game.

Getting that college degree. Getting married. Starting a new career. Though we may make all kinds of excuses, it's often never too late for life-changing decisions and milestones.

This is especially true in our faith life, which is based on God's promises through Jesus Christ. He showed up in Bethany four days late, as Martha pointed out, having seemingly dawdled a little as though the death of his friend Lazarus really didn't matter to him. It clearly did since he broke down and cried when he saw Lazarus' burial site. Being Jesus, however, he wasn't late; he was right on time because with Jesus there are no impossible situations or circumstances.

This is true in our own lives no matter how hopeless our current circumstances may appear to us. At any time – today even -- we can regret the things we have done wrong and the way we have lived, ask God in Jesus' name to forgive us for them, and discover a new way of living – forever.

With Jesus, it's never too late.

I reminded our guys all year how badly we wanted to play in '04.
-- Graduate assistant Travis Williams on the BCS title game

It's never too late to change a life
by turning it over to Jesus.

DAY 16

GOOD JOB

Read Matthew 25:14-30.

"His master replied, 'Well done, good and faithful servant!'" (v. 21)

Watson Downs knew he had to do a good job in a hurry because he didn't get many chances.

The Auburn coaches invited Downs to walk on as a quarterback in 2008. Before he arrived on campus, though, he talked the situation over with his high school coach and decided the defensive side of the ball might be a better fit for him. "I had played a little linebacker during my senior year . . ., and I wasn't afraid of the contact," he said. So in the summer of 2008, Downs walked on as a linebacker.

He redshirted that season and then got some playing time in three games in 2009. He wound up on national television during the Tigers' 54-30 win over Ball State, but the game was not exactly the highlight of his football career, yielding him a nickname he would just as soon discard. The omnipresent TV cameras caught Downs getting very thoroughly chewed out by head coach Gene Chizik after he drew a penalty for a late hit right in front of the coaches on the sideline. After that, punter Clinton Durst tagged him with the moniker "Out of Bounds Downs." "It looked like he was still in [bounds] when I hit him," Downs said in his defense.

Downs saw limited action during the national championship season at linebacker and on special teams. His most extensive

TIGERS

playing time came in the 62-24 romp over Chattanooga on Nov. 7. He expected to see some action since the Tigers were heavy favorites; indeed, they led 27-0 after the first quarter. What Downs didn't know was how much he would get to play.

It turned out he played quite a bit, on the field for the majority of the last half. With one shot at doing a good job, he made the most of it. He recorded five tackles, tying freshmen Ryan White, Demetruce McNeal, and Jake Holland for second on the team. Linebacker Eltoro Freeman led the defense with eight stops.

For Watson Downs, it was a good job indeed.

Well done. Way to go. They are words that make us all swell up a little like a puffer fish and smile no matter how hard we try not to. We may deny it in an honest attempt to be at least reasonably humble, but we all cherish praise. We work hard and we may be well rewarded for it financially, but a cold, hard paycheck is not always enough. We like to be told we're doing something well; we desire to be appreciated.

Nowhere, however, is that affirmation more important than when it comes from God himself. We will all meet God one day, which is intimidating even to consider. How our soul will ring with unspeakable joy on that day of days if we hear God's thundering voice say to us, "Well done, good and faithful servant."

Could anything else really matter other than doing a good job for God?

You're just grateful for the opportunity of just being on the team.
-- Watson Downs after the 2010 Chattanooga game.

If we don't do a good job for God in our lives,
all our work amounts to nothing.

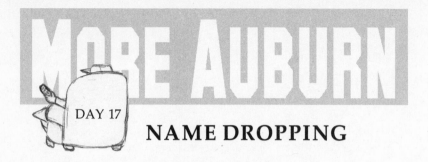

DAY 17

NAME DROPPING

Read Exodus 3:13-20.

"God said to Moses, 'I AM WHO I AM. This is what you are to say to the Israelites: 'I AM has sent me to you'" *(v. 14).*

If there is a better 1950s football name than Zeke Smith, I've never heard it. It's Disneyian." So declared one writer about the Auburn gridiron legend. But, of course, "Zeke" was a nickname.

Roger Duane Smith needed some help from an Alabama alum to wind up at Auburn. He played fullback at a small school, and an Alabama graduate in town tried to get his school to look at Smith. When the Tide wasn't interested, he talked to Auburn. Head coach Shug Jordan gave him one of his last scholarships.

Even in high school, he was "Zeke" Smith. The moniker was slapped upon him by his high school football coach because of his fondness for Zeke Bratkowski, an All-American quarterback for Georgia in 1952 and '53. Interestingly, "Zeke" wasn't Bratkowski's real name; it was Edmund Raymond.

Jordan wasn't sure what do with Smith, but he knew he wasn't a college back, so the freshman played as a substitute center in 1955. "At first I missed playing in the backfield," Smith said. "But I just wanted to play."

After Smith was redshirted in 1956, Jordan made a decision that helped changed Auburn football history. He moved the sophomore to guard, and he immediately won a starting job on both sides of the line for the 1957 national championship team.

Zeke Smith went on to win the Outland Trophy in 1958 as the country's best interior lineman. He was All-America as a junior and as a senior. Each year, the Zeke Smith Award is presented to Auburn's Defensive Player of the Year.

Nicknames such as "Zeke" are not slapped haphazardly upon individuals but rather reflect widely held perceptions about the person named or say something about the individual. Proper names do that also.

Nowhere throughout history has this concept been more prevalent than in the Bible, where a name is not a mere label but is an expression of the essential nature of the named one. That is, a person's name reveals his or her character. Even God shares this concept; to know the name of God is to know God as he has chosen to reveal himself to us.

What does your name say about you? Honest, trustworthy, a seeker of the truth and a person of God? Or does the mention of your name cause your coworkers to whisper snide remarks, your neighbors to roll their eyes, or your friends to start making allowances for you?

Most importantly, what does your name say about you to God? He, too, knows you by name.

I guess that name will stick with me forever. Not too many people call me Roger. Nobody does but my mother.

-- Roger Duane "Zeke" Smith

**Live so that your name evokes
positive associations by people you know,
by the public, and by God.**

DAY 18

THE ANSWER

Read Colossians 2:2-10.

"My purpose is that they . . . may know the mystery of God, namely, Christ, in whom are hidden all the treasures of wisdom and knowledge" (vv. 2, 3).

Ole Miss had an answer for Cam Newton's rushing ability. Fortunately, Auburn had an answer for the Rebs' answer.

The 8-0 and top-ranked Tigers went over to Vaught-Hemingway Stadium on Oct. 30, 2010, for what was billed as a trap game. At 3-4, the Rebs weren't that good but they weren't that bad either. Also, the Tigers were coming off their biggest win of the season, the 24-17 whipping of 6th-ranked and undefeated LSU.

Newton went into the game with 1,077 yards rushing, already the most in SEC history for a quarterback. The Ole Miss coaches were determined he would not beat them running the ball, and they came up with an answer that worked. The Rebs loaded the line of scrimmage; their defensive ends stayed on the perimeter, and they dedicated a linebacker to follow Newton wherever he went. As a result, they held Newton to only 45 yards rushing, virtually eliminating him from the game as a running threat.

Offensive coordinator Gus Malzahn simply came up with his own answer, and it worked really well. Newton morphed into a more traditional quarterback who threw the ball and handed off to his tailbacks. The result was 572 yards of total offense and a 51-31 romp that wasn't as close as the score might indicate.

Newton started throwing from the get-go, hitting 15 of 21 passes for 188 yards in the first half. At the break, Auburn was up 34-17. He threw only three more passes, turning the game over to his tailbacks the last half. Michael Dyer rushed for 188 yards in the game; Onterio McCalebb had 99 yards.

Ultimately, Ole Miss had no answer for the offensive adjustments the Tigers made.

Experience is essentially the uncovering of answers to some of life's questions, both trivial and profound. You often discover that as soon as you learn a few answers, the questions change. Your children get older, your health worsens, your financial situation changes, one of Auburn's teams struggles unexpectedly -- all situations requiring answers to a new set of difficulties.

No answers, though, are more important than the ones you seek in your search for God and the meaning of life because they determine your fate for all eternity. Since a life of faith is a journey and not a destination, the questions do indeed change with your circumstances. The "why" or the "what" you ask God when you're a teenager is vastly different from the quandaries you ponder as an adult.

No matter how you phrase the question, though, the answer inevitably centers on Jesus. And that answer never changes.

Tonight they did a nice job of taking Cameron away, and we had to work other avenues.
-- Gene Chizik on finding an answer to the Ole Miss defense

It doesn't matter what the question is;
if it has to do with life, temporal or eternal,
the answer lies in Jesus.

DAY 19

IMPRESSIONS

Read John 1:1-18.

"In the beginning was the Word, and the Word was with God, and the Word was God. . . . The Word became flesh and made his dwelling among us" (vv. 1, 14).

T'Sharvan Bell spent his sophomore season trying to eradicate from his coaches' minds the impression he had made on them his freshman year.

In 2009, Bell "got stuck with the nastiest label a defensive back could have." The Auburn coaches believed he was "soft." They felt he was "a tad bit timid, maybe even a little scared at times."

Bell didn't appreciate that assessment one bit, so he decided he would create a new impression. He went to work to fashion a new image, arriving early for and staying late at practice and never passing up a chance to show the coaches just how tough he was.

By the start of the 2010 season, Bell was the first backup for both cornerback spots. A month into the season, head coach Gene Chizik said he was "basically a starter."

Bell created a permanent new impression with one big play in the Iron Bowl. Late in the game, the coaches called his number. Auburn led 28-27, but Alabama was driving into sight of a field goal. On third down, defensive coordinator Ted Roof called for Bell to blitz on the right side of the Alabama defense.

He timed his rush perfectly, slipping past a would-be blocker. He grabbed the quarterback by the arm to "get the ball out," but when he couldn't, he swung him to the ground. The sack pushed Alabama out of field-goal range and preserved the win.

Earlier in the game, Bell made another play that showed just how tough he was. On a first-and-goal, Alabama ran a sweep and appeared to have a touchdown. Bell ripped through two blockers, though, and dropped the runner for a yard loss. On the next snap, Nick Fairley forced and recovered a fumble, a play he never would have made had not the once-soft Bell made his play.

That guy in the apartment next door. A job search complete with interview. A twenty-year class reunion. The new neighbors. As T'Sharvan Bell was with his coaches, we are constantly about the fraught task of wanting to make an impression on people. We want them to remember us, obviously in a flattering way.

We make that impression, good or bad, generally in two ways. Even with instant communication on the Internet – perhaps especially with the Internet – we primarily influence the opinion others have of us by our words. After that, we can advance to the next level by making an impression with our actions.

God gave us an impression of himself in exactly the same way. In Jesus, God took the unprecedented step of appearing to mortals as one of us, as mere flesh and bone. We now know for all time the sorts of things God does and the sorts of things God says. In Jesus, God put his divine foot forward to make a good impression on each one of us.

I took it personal. I really did.
  -- T'Sharvan Bell on the initial impression his coaches had of him

**Through Jesus' words and actions,
God seeks to impress us with his love.**

DAY 20

ON CALL

Read 1 Samuel 3:1-18.

"The Lord came and stood there, calling as at the other times, 'Samuel! Samuel!' Then Samuel said, 'Speak, for your servant is listening'" (v. 10).

With his team in trouble, Shug Jordan answered the call and rescued what turned out to be a championship season.

Ralph "Shug" Jordan is, of course, best known as the Hall-of-Fame head coach of the Auburn Tigers who led them to 176 wins, including the 1957 national title over 25 seasons. But Jordan was also an outstanding athlete, lettering in football, baseball, and basketball at Auburn. As a senior in 1932, he was named the school's Most Outstanding Athlete.

Jordan was on the varsity baseball squad for three seasons, seeing action mostly as a utility fielder. Prior to his senior season, he had started only one game as a pitcher.

But Auburn's aces, Clifford Smith and Ripper Williams, both took ill, and the team was coming off a road trip that had used up a lot of the pitching arms. They had won the old Dixie League title the season before, but were only 3-3 with the Florida Gators headed to town for a big two-game series.

As Jordan recalled it, the head coach told him to show his stuff. He threw two pitches, and the coach said, "You got it, Lefty. Get in there." So Shug Jordan answered the call.

Porter Grant, a lifelong friend of Jordan's who later coached

TIGERS

baseball at Auburn, always said "every inning was two outs, three and two on the batter, and the bases loaded. He claim[ed] Florida had twenty-seven men left on base."

It wasn't much of an exaggeration. Jordan won the game 5-2, but Florida smacked eleven hits and left thirteen men on base. A writer said Jordan was "invincible with Floridians on the basepath." Florida loaded the bases in the ninth before Grant bailed out his buddy with a great catch in center field for the final out.

Jordan's clutch performance sparked the entire team. They didn't lose again, finishing 13-3, and won the Dixie League title.

A team player is someone such as Shug Jordan who does whatever the coach calls upon him to do to help out the team. Something quite similar occurs when God places a specific call upon a Christian's life.

This is much scarier, though, than being called on to pitch. The way many folks understand it is that answering God's call means going into the ministry, packing the family up, and moving halfway around the world to some place where folks have never heard of air conditioning, fried chicken, paved roads, or the Tigers. Zambia. The Philippines. Cleveland even.

Not for you, no thank you. And who can blame you?

But God usually calls folks to serve him where they are. In fact, God put you where you are right now, and he has a purpose in placing you there. Wherever you are, you are called to serve him.

I was an atrocious pitcher.
— Shug Jordan on answering the call against Florida

God calls you to serve him right now
right where he has put you, wherever that is.

DAY 21

THE PANIC BUTTON

Read Mark 4:35-41.

"He said to his disciples, 'Why are you so afraid? Do you still have no faith?'" (v. 40)

If the Tigers ever had an opportunity or a reason to panic, half-time at Alabama [in 2004] seemed to be a good time for it."

The undefeated, third-ranked Tigers didn't seem to feel the pressure of their lofty status the week leading up to the Iron Bowl. "The one thing about this team is that they have fun," said head coach Tommy Tuberville. "They'll enjoy going to Tuscaloosa."

The Tigers may have enjoyed the trip, but they certainly didn't relish the first half. Only strong play from the defense kept the initial thirty minutes from being an unmitigated disaster. The Tiger offense produced minus-four yards on its first three possessions. Linebacker Kevin Sears intercepted a Tide pass at the one-yard line to help keep the score close. Despite being totally dominated, Auburn trailed only 6-0 at the break.

This was the first time all season the eventual SEC champs had been down at halftime. Nevertheless, the Auburn locker room showed no trace of panic. "The kids were relatively calm," and so were the coaches, said strength coach Kevin Yoxall. "Both coordinators talked to the kids about how they were going to fix [the problems]. There never was a sense of people ranting and raving."

The coaches did offer a plan to get the offense moving. It worked. On the first series of the half, the Tigers drove for a touchdown.

TIGERS

The big play was a 51-yard completion from Jason Campbell to wide receiver Devin Aromashodu down to the Alabama 5-yard line. On the next play, tailback Carnell Williams scored.

After that, if there were any trace of panic anywhere around, it lay on the Alabama side of the field. The Tigers scored 21 straight points and completed an undefeated season with a 21-13 win.

Have you ever experienced that suffocating sensation of fear escalating into full-blown panic? Maybe the time when you couldn't find your child at the mall or at the beach? Or the heart-stopping moment when you looked out and saw that tornado headed your way?

As the disciples illustrate, the problem with panic is that it debilitates us. Here they were, with some professional fishermen among them, and they let a bad storm panic them into helplessness. All they could do was wake up an exhausted Jesus.

We shouldn't be too hard on them, though, because we often make an even more grievous mistake. They panicked and turned to Jesus; we panic and often turn away from Jesus by underestimating both his power and his ability to handle our crises.

We have a choice when fear clutches us: We can assume Jesus no longer cares for us, surrender to it, and descend into panic, or we can remember how much Jesus loves us and resist fear and panic by trusting in him.

The Tigers behaved as if they had been there before and knew just what to do.
-- Writer Richard Scott on the lack of panic in the Auburn locker room

To panic is to believe – wrongly -- that Jesus is incapable of handling the crises in our lives.

DAY 22

CASE OF THE NERVES

Read Mark 5:1-20.

"What do you want with me, Jesus, Son of the Most High God? Swear to God that you won't torture me!" (v. 7)

Brandon Mosley's career at Auburn really started on a day when he was so nervous that another player felt he had to step in and help him out.

A junior college transfer, Mosley played tackle for the Tigers in 2010 and 2011. He started 24 straight games and appeared in all 27 games those two seasons. He was second-team All-SEC as a senior. As a junior, he started the last eleven games and was part of the line that cleared the way for the offense to set a school record by rushing for 300 yards or more in six consecutive SEC games on the way to the national championship.

Along with practically everyone else, Mosley saw some action in the 2010 season opener, a 52-26 blowout of Arkansas State. The opponent the following Thursday night, though, was Mississippi State, so Mosley didn't expect to see much, if any, playing time. He was so sure he wouldn't play tackle that he wore jersey number 84 on the sideline, a receiver's number since he had been asked by the coaches to help out at tight end.

Early on, though, All-American tackle Lee Ziemba, who would win the Jacobs Blocking Trophy as the best blocker in the league, went down with an injury. After missing a play while he hunted for his number 75 jersey, Mosley rushed onto the field where the reality of the situation hit him. "When (Mosley) came in, he looked pretty nervous," said guard Mike Berry. So Berry took the situation in hand. "I just told him: Listen to me. I'm going to help you with the calls."

"My main concern was just not messing up," Mosley said. Once he settled down, he did quite well, displaying the exceptionally quick feet that helped him eventually move into the starting line-up and become a star. His nervousness disappeared for good.

We often can't really explain why some situations make us nervous. Delivering a speech, for instance. Or being around a person we'd like to ask out.

We probably rarely -- if ever -- consider the possibility that we make other people nervous. Who in the world could be intimidated by us? Try this on for starters: Satan himself. Yep, that very demon of darkness that Hollywood repeatedly portrays as so powerful that goodness is helpless before him. That's the one.

But we can make Satan nervous only if we stand before him with the power of Jesus Christ at our disposal. As Christians, we seem to understand that our basic mission is to further Jesus' kingdom and change the world through emulating him in the way we live and love others. But do we appreciate that in truly living for Jesus, we are daily tormenting the very devil himself?

Satan and his lackeys quake helplessly in fear and nervousness before the power of almighty God that is in us through Jesus.

His eyes were big and stuff.
-- Guard Mike Berry on how nervous Brandon Mosley was

Nervous and apprehensive -- so stands Satan himself in the presence of a follower of Jesus.

BAD IDEA

Read Mark 14:43-50.

"The betrayer had arranged a signal with them: 'The one I kiss is the man; arrest him and lead him away under guard'" (v. 44).

Here's a good idea. For the largest crowd in the state's football history, bring in a powerhouse team to ensure a good, exciting game. Funny thing about that.

The 9-1-1 Tigers of 1987 won the SEC title outright. They shut out Alabama 10-0 and pounded Georgia 27-11 and Florida 29-6. Outside linebacker Aundray Bruce was the SEC Defensive Player of the Year. For the first time in school history four players were honored as first-team All-America: Bruce, defensive tackle Tracy Rocker, offensive tackle Stacy Searels, and linebacker Kurt Crain.

An expansion that made Jordan-Hare the fifth largest on-campus stadium in the country was completed in the off-season. The $15.5-million project raised the facility's capacity to 85,187. Added were more than 10,000 upper-level seats and 71 executive suites plus various amenities such as a Letterman's Lounge.

AU head coach and athletic director Pat Dye decided to scratch the season-opening game originally scheduled against Chattanooga and bring in a perennial power for the occasion. Dye's plan appeared to work when Texas agreed to come to Auburn. Also expecting a thrilling game, ESPN televised the game nationally.

It was a good idea, all right. It's just that Texas didn't do its part. The Tigers slaughtered the Longhorns 31-3, handing them the worst opening-day loss in the program's storied history.

On the game's sixth play, Bruce pressured the Texas quarterback into throwing an interception to cornerback Alvin Briggs. On the second play, AU quarterback Jeff Burger, who was 16 of 22 passing for the day, flipped a 23-yard pass to wide receiver Duke Donaldson. Two plays later, fullback Reggie Ware scored.

The game wasn't even four minutes old, and the rout was on.

That sure-fire investment you made from a pal's hot stock tip. The expensive exercise machine that now traps dust bunnies under your bed. Blond hair. Telling your wife you wanted to eat at the restaurant with the waitresses in the skimpy shorts. They seemed like pretty good ideas at the time; they weren't.

We all have bad ideas in our lifetime. They provide some of our most crucial learning experiences.

Some ideas, though, are so irreparably and inherently bad that we cannot help but wonder why they were even conceived in the first place. Almost two thousand years ago a man had just such an idea. Judas' betrayal of Jesus remains to this day one of the most heinous acts of treachery in history.

Turning his back on Jesus was a bad idea for Judas then; it's a bad idea for us now.

You cannot overestimate the impact of the enlarged stadium on our program.
— Pat Dye on what a good idea expanding Jordan-Hare was

We all have some pretty bad ideas
during our lifetime, but nothing equals
the folly of turning away from Jesus.

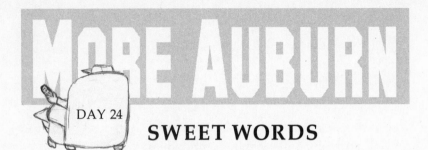

DAY 24

SWEET WORDS

Read Romans 8:28-39.

"'In all these things we are more than conquerors through him who loved us (v. 37).

After a costly turnover late in the BCS championship game, Cam Newton wasn't feeling too good about himself. Offensive coordinator Gus Malzahn was ready, though, with some affirmation for his team's leader.

Top-ranked Auburn met the second-ranked Oregon Ducks in Glendale AZ on Jan. 10, 2011, for the national championship. The pundits predicted a battle of offensive juggernauts who would spend the night lighting up the scoreboard. It didn't turn out that way at all; instead, it was the defenses that dominated.

In the process, thanks largely to the Oregon defense, Newton did not have one of his best games; the Ducks limited him to 64 yards rushing on 22 carries. Newton's worst moment of the night, though, came late in the fourth quarter. With less than five minutes to play, the Tigers led 19-11 and had the ball; the national championship was pretty much theirs to lose -- and they almost did. Newton coughed up a fumble that gave Oregon the ball at its own 45. Eight plays later, the Ducks scored and converted a two-point try. With 2:33 to play, the game was tied.

Malzahn knew exactly what his quarterback needed as he trotted off the field after the devastating fumble. Malzahn, who left the Plains for the head job at Arkansas State after the 2011 season, went right to his star with some affirmation. "Hey, man, he said, "you got us here. Keep your head up, 'cause you're gonna help us to win it."

Newton, of course, did just that. After the kickoff, he quarterbacked the Tigers on the game-winning drive that ended with Wes Byrum's field goal and the 22-19 final score.

You make a key decision. All excited, you tell your best friend or spouse and await a reaction. "Boy, that was dumb" is the answer you get. A friend's life spirals out of control into a total disaster. Do you pretend you don't know that messed-up person?

Even as Cam Newton did in the championship game, everybody needs affirmation in some degree. That is, we all occasionally need someone to say something positive about us, that we are worth something, and that God loves us.

The follower of Jesus does what our Lord did when he encountered someone whose life was a mess. Rather than seeing what they were, he saw what they could become. Life is hard; it breaks us all to some degree. To be like Jesus, we see past the problems of the broken and the hurting and envision their potential, understanding that not condemning is not condoning.

The Christian's words of affirmation are the greatest and most joyous of all. They constitute a message of victory and triumph in Jesus from which nothing can separate us or defeat us.

You can motivate football players better with kind words than you can with a whip.
> *-- Legendary college football coach Bud Wilkinson*

**The greatest way to affirm lost persons
is to lead them to Christ.**

TEST CASE

Read James 1:2-12.

"Blessed is the man who perseveres under trial, because when he has stood the test, he will receive the crown of life that God has promised to those who love him" (v. 12).

For fleeting minutes, Auburn gymnast Sarah Wentworth's life couldn't have been much better." Her joy and triumph, though, would almost immediately "be trumped by despair" and her "faith would be tested as it had never been tested before."

As a senior in 2000, Wentworth was the SEC Gymnast of the Year. She still holds the school record for the three highest scores on the uneven bars.

On March 5, 2000, she nailed a perfect 10 on the uneven bars. Minutes later, though, she landed awkwardly on a vault, and the damage was devastating. She hyperextended both knees so badly that she tore the ACL's in both knees, ruptured a joint, and broke a leg. "I knew it was over," she said.

But "a broken leg and two mangled knees would be the least of Wentworth's worries before the night was over." She rejected her parents' offer to ride in the car with them back to Auburn, figuring she would have more room on the team bus and would have ice available. On the trip home, an 18-wheeler slammed into the Wentworths' vehicle. Had Sarah been in the back seat, she would have certainly been killed. Her mom suffered a broken leg; her dad's neck was broken.

Back in Auburn, Wentworth didn't know about the accident. As a doctor examined her, he received a note and passed it on to her. It said only, "Parents in BAD accident. Mom broken leg. Dad broken neck." "That's all he got," Wentworth said.

But she had given her life to Christ her sophomore year at Auburn, and she relied on her faith to calm her. "I just knew things were going to be OK," she said. And they were.

She never felt any bitterness about the premature end of her career, saying, "I just knew it was time for me to be finished."

Her faith won out on the night she was tested.

Life often seems to be one battery of tests after another: high-school and college final exams, college entrance exams, the driver's license test, professional certification exams. They all stress us out because they measure our competency, and we fear that we will be found wanting.

But it is the tests in our lives that don't involve paper and pen that often demand the most of us. That is, like Sarah Wentworth, we regularly run headlong into challenges, obstacles, barriers, and heartache that test our abilities, our persistence, and our faith.

Life itself is one long test, which means some parts are bound to be hard. Viewing life as an ongoing exam may help you keep your sanity, your perspective, and your faith when troubles come your way. After all, God is the proctor, but he isn't neutral. He even gave you the answer you need to pass with flying colors; that answer is "Jesus."

It's kind of like God's grace. You don't deserve it, but it's given to you.
-- Sarah Wentworth on having a gymnastics award named after her

Life is a test that God wants you to ace.

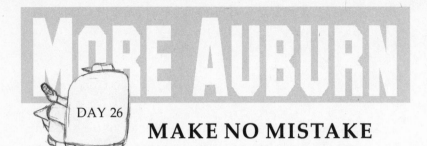

DAY 26

MAKE NO MISTAKE

Read Mark 14:66-72.

"Then Peter remembered the word Jesus had spoken to him: 'Before the rooster crows twice you will disown me three times.' And he broke down and wept" (v. 72).

Two straight mistakes left the Tigers in trouble in the fourth quarter. Fortunately, South Carolina decided to make a slew of mistakes of its own.

On Sept. 25, 2010, 17th-ranked Auburn hosted 12th-ranked USC in an early-season battle of challengers for the two league division titles. Carolina led 27-21 after three quarters. In the final period, the Tigers drove to a fourth down at the Gamecock 1 and decided to go for it. Then came a pair of crucial mistakes.

The first miscue was a false-start penalty that forced a field-goal try. But Wes Byrum, who would, of course, chisel his name deep into Auburn lore with his game-winning kick against Oregon, clanked it. The two miscues meant the Tigers still trailed.

But Carolina suddenly couldn't hold onto the ball. The Gamecocks' last four possessions of the game all resulted in turnovers. Defensive back T'Sharvan Bell recovered a fumble, tackle Mike Blanc did the same, linebacker Josh Bynes intercepted a pass, and cornerback Demond Washington also nabbed one.

The Tigers took advantage of all that self-inflicted carnage to score a pair of touchdowns. After the first Carolina mistake, Cam Newton tossed a 7-yard touchdown pass to Philip Lutzenkirchen for a 28-27 lead. After the second fumble, Newton and Emory Blake teamed up for a 12-yard TD on a screen pass. The final of 35-27 was on the board with 6:23 to play.

USC head coach Steve Spurrier changed quarterbacks after the two fumbles. It didn't help because the sub then made his own mistakes by throwing two interceptions, both of which ended USC threats deep in Auburn territory.

It's distressing but it's true: Like football teams and Simon Peter, we all make mistakes. Only one perfect man ever walked on this earth, and no one of us is he. Some mistakes are just dumb. Like locking yourself out of your car or falling into a swimming pool with your clothes on.

Other mistakes are more significant. Like heading down a path to addiction. Committing a crime. Walking out on a spouse and the children.

All these mistakes, however, from the momentarily annoying to the life-altering tragic, share one aspect: They can all be forgiven in Christ. Other folks may not forgive us; we may not even forgive ourselves. But God will forgive us when we call upon him in Jesus' name.

Thus, the twofold fatal mistake we can make is ignoring the fact that we will die one day and subsequently ignoring the fact that Jesus is the only way to shun Hell and enter Heaven. We absolutely must get this one right.

Turnovers are strange things. Sometimes they come in bunches.
-- Gene Chizik on USC's four fourth-quarter mistakes

Only one mistake we make sends us to Hell
when we die: ignoring Jesus while we live.

FOOLPROOF

Read 1 Corinthians 1:18-31.

"For the message of the cross is foolishness to those who are perishing, but to us who are being saved it is the power of God" (v. 18).

Auburn cornerback Carlos Rogers was so bored on the football field that he often tried all sorts of foolishness just to get a quarterback to throw his way.

Following the undefeated 2004 season, Rogers, a senior, won the Jim Thorpe Award as the nation's best defensive back. An All-America that year, he was a four-year starter who set the school record with forty pass deflections.

Rogers honestly didn't think he would win the Thorpe Award. That's because he just didn't have the gaudy numbers that most award winners roll up. There was a very good reason for that: Nobody would throw his way.

"Carlos is a lock-down corner who can play a whole half of the field by himself," linebacker Travis Williams said about his teammate. "No one would throw at him -- that's respect."

In the SEC championship season of 2004, opponents threw only 65 passes in Rogers' general direction the whole year. As a result, he spent a lot of time on the field watching the action and being downright bored.

"The quarterbacks would just turn and look the other way," Rogers said. So he began to try a little foolishness just to get some balls thrown in his direction. For instance, he would leave his man open a bit hoping to bait the quarterback into a pass. Sometimes he would throw his hands up in the air, jump up and down, and wave his arms over his head in an attempt to fool the quarterback into thinking he was an open receiver.

The truth was, though, that his tricks and his foolishness didn't help much. He was just too good to fool anybody.

Our culture proclaims that right now is all there is; hey, let's live for today with no worries about cause and effect. Many of us buy into that philosophy. Congress recklessly spends money the nation doesn't have. Like a mini-version of our legislators, we load up our credit cards far beyond our abilities to sustain. We treat our bodies as though we will never suffer any repercussions for drugs and alcohol or even for a lousy diet and no exercise.

So to live with an eye not only on tomorrow but on eternity is foolishness to the world. To regard our actions as having eternal consequences – what's up with that? And to believe that we are responsible for where we spend life after death – to believe in an afterlife at all -- how foolish is that?

It's as foolish as almighty God himself, he who died on the cross to loose his saving power on a lost world overly prideful of its own foolish wisdom.

It is foolish to expect a young man to follow your advice and to ignore your example.

-- Basketball coach Don Meyer

Through Jesus, God has turned our notions
of wisdom and foolishness inside out
and upside down.

DAY 28

OUT OF CHARACTER

Read Mark 6:1-6.

"'Isn't this Mary's son, and the brother of James, Joseph, Judas and Simon. Aren't his sisters here with us?' And they took offense at him" (v. 3).

Lee Ziemba said his sudden metamorphosis into a cheerleader was no big deal. His surprised teammates disagreed.

Ziemba was the most decorated of the linemen on the 2010 national championship team. The left tackle, he was All-America and won the Jacobs Blocking Trophy as the SEC's best blocker. He set the school record by starting fifty-two consecutive games.

Ziemba led by example and effort; he didn't feel the need to get into his teammates' faces and yell and scream to motivate them. He was "an introspective guy" whose attitude was "You handle your business and I'll handle mine." He said he didn't like to lecture, rant, or rave, "because we all know what the speech is going to say."

But in the Kentucky game of Oct. 9, Ziemba and his Tiger teammates found themselves right smack dab in the midst of times that try men's souls. Especially football players.

Auburn had just lost its lead in the game for the second time. With an undefeated season on the line, the score was tied at 34, the fourth quarter was half over, and the Tigers had the ball on their own 7-yard line. These were desperate times, and Ziemba, the introspective one, "began to feel the fire." He didn't like the way

TIGERS

the offense was quiet; it was time for somebody to say something, to become the rah-ray guy and get the offense fired up.

So Lee Ziemba, the most unlikely cheerleader of them all, spoke up. "I felt like I needed to say something," he said. "It wasn't a big deal." But it was.

Ziemba's fiery, heartfelt 30-second plea to his teammates spawned a 19-play drive that ended with a field goal and a 37-34 Auburn win. Quarterback Cam Newton had no doubt that the credit for the drive's inspiration lay with his left tackle.

Over time, people who know you expect you to behave a certain way. Thus, you totally flummox your friends and family members when you haul off and do something out of character as Lee Ziemba did to his teammates in the Kentucky game by becoming the cheerleader for the offense. In your case, maybe you bought a flashy new car, got your hair cut short or changed the color altogether, or suddenly switched careers.

Maybe you even reinvigorated or discovered your faith life.

Acting out of character when it comes to your faith is exactly what you want to do. It is, in fact, the most revealing mark of a person who is serious about his or her walk with Jesus, whether it's a new hiker or an experienced trekker taking the trip.

That's because the goal for a Christian really is a change in character. You seek not to act like yourself anymore. Rather, you emulate the ideal. You act like Jesus instead.

What was new to a lot of people's ears was Lee Ziemba's pep talk.
— Cam Newton

To be serious about Jesus is to act out of character; rather than acting like yourself, you act like him.

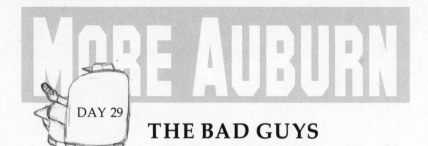

DAY 29

THE BAD GUYS

Read Ephesians 6:10-18.

*"Our struggle is not against flesh and blood, but against
the rulers, against the authorities, against the powers of
this dark world and against the spiritual forces of evil in
the heavenly realms" (v. 12).*

The players were "hoodlums," the coaches were "deep-dyed
scoundrel[s]", and the game was "mental idleness to the participant." What awful, evil sport was this? Auburn football.

The Tigers fielded their first football team in 1892, but not everybody was happy about this new game that became the rage on
college campuses across the nation. In 1897, the *Birmingham News*
called for "abolishing this inhuman sport" that was "more brutal
than prize fighting and a greater menace to human life."

In 1903, L.S. Boyd, an Auburn man, wrote and distributed a
football pamphlet that deplored the game at his alma mater. In
calling for the Alabama legislature to outlaw the game, he said,
"Football is mental idleness to the participant and insanity to all of
the student body." Boyd asserted that football players "absolutely
disregard all college discipline" and were under the control of a
coach who "in most cases cannot make a living at anything else,
and in a majority of cases is a man of loose morals, and very often
a deep-dyed scoundrel as well."

Boyd blamed a fickle public for worshipping "at the shrine of
our insane and worthless system of college athletics." He declared

TIGERS

that since athletics had begun at Auburn "the standard of scholarship has been lowered; the religious activities have declined; . . . and a general spirit of carelessness and frivolity has supplanted the seriousness and sober-mindedness of the olden time."

In other words, football was downright evil and football players and coaches were the bad guys.

More than a century later, we still have trouble identifying the exact nature of the evil swirling around us, though we're pretty confident it isn't the Auburn football players and coaches. We do know that a just and good God tolerates the existence of evil even if why this is so remains a mystery.

Evil is not intrinsically a part of God's physical world, which God declared to be "good." Rather, evil is a function of the spirit world, of Satan and his minions. Human beings are thus the pawns in an ongoing cosmic struggle between good and evil. The primary battleground is our hearts. This is why we struggle with evil even after we surrender our lives to Christ. The forces of evil don't concede defeat; they just work harder and longer.

The day of God's own choosing will come when all evil will be defeated and goodness will rule unopposed. Not only will the spiritual forces of evil be eradicated, but so will those humans who have aligned themselves with them. Evil is for losers.

The modern college student has about as much respect for religious matters as an intelligent billy-goat.
-- L.S. Boyd on the evils resulting from college athletics

Evil may win temporarily – even in your heart –
but to follow Jesus is to live daily
in the knowledge of good's ultimate triumph.

DAY 30

YOU NEVER KNOW

Read Judges 6:11-23.

"'But Lord,' Gideon asked, 'how can I save Israel? My clan is the weakest in Manasseh, and I am the least in my family'" (v. 15).

What the 1957 Auburn football team did illustrates one of the sport's most abiding and exciting truths: You never know what's going to happen until you suit up and play the games.

Even when it was over and the national title was theirs after an undefeated season, many of the players didn't know they had won anything. "Somebody told somebody else and they told me" is how quarterback Lloyd Nix learned his team was officially the best in all of college football. Nix never even knew whether or not the students and fans rolled Toomer's Corner in celebration. (Buster Gross, a student coach on the 1957 squad, said they did after an Associated Press editor formally presented the national championship trophy to the Tigers on Dec. 10.)

Such downright indifference about the national championship is simply unimaginable today. But this was 1957, long before the age of the Internet, ESPN, and talk radio. Unlike the march of the 2010 team to the title, "no one fretted much about Auburn and the '57 title, at least inside the Tiger football team."

That included the coaches. As Gross recalled, "We knew the '57 team was something special. But still, the coaches didn't realize they were in contention to win the national championship until

TIGERS

right at the end of the season." Head coach Shug Jordan didn't even mention the prospect to his team until right before the Iron Bowl, a 40-0 Auburn win. He simply said, "Guys, if y'all have a good game, you have a chance of being a national champion."

They did -- and they were -- even if they didn't know it.

You never know what you can do until – like the Tigers of 1957 -- you want to bad enough or until – like Gideon -- you have to because God insists. Serving in the military, maybe even in combat. Standing by a friend while everyone else unjustly excoriates her. Undergoing agonizing medical treatment and managing to smile. You never know what life will demand of you.

It's that way too in your relationship with God. As Gideon discovered to his dismay, you never know what God will ask of you. You can know that God expects you to be faithful; thus, you must be willing to trust him even when he calls you to tasks that appear daunting and beyond your abilities.

You can respond faithfully and confidently to whatever God it is calls you to do for him. That's because even though you never know what lies ahead, you can know with absolutely certainty that God will lead you and will provide what you need. As it was with the Israelites, God will never lead you into the wilderness and then leave you there.

They announced [the national title] to the team, and that night they took us out to a nice restaurant out of town for a big dinner.
– Buster Gross on the lack of hoopla in 1957

You never know what God will ask you to do,
but you always know he will
provide everything you need to do it.

DAY 31

BIG DEAL

Read Ephesians 3:1-13.

"His intent was that now, through the church, the manifold wisdom of God should be made known" (v. 10).

Being behind was no big deal for the 2010 Tigers, but being 24 points down in the game that was the most important of them all was a very big deal.

No matter how the rest of the season unfolds, the Iron Bowl is always the season's biggest deal. In 2010, it certainly was. To keep their national title hopes alive, the second-ranked Tigers had to get past the ninth-ranked Tide. No Auburn fan could have envisioned the nightmare that the first half turned out to be.

The Tigers had trailed Clemson by 17 points, South Carolina by 13, and Georgia by 14, and they, of course, had won all three games with stirring comebacks. So Alabama led 24-0 after a start of which offensive coordinator Gus Malzahn said, "We were on the verge of being terrible." He was perhaps being kind seeing as how Alabama led 21-0 before Auburn even had a first down.

But apparently, this, too, was no big deal, for what followed was a comeback that will live forever in the hearts and souls of the Auburn family. Writer Austin Murphy described Auburn's play in the final 30 minutes as "astonishing."

Perhaps the biggest play of the Tiger comeback took place in the second quarter. Heisman-Trophy winner Mark Ingram was on his way to a touchdown that would up the Tide lead to 28-0 when

TIGERS

senior defensive end Antoine Carter overtook him and punched the ball loose. The pigskin incredibly shot forward for 30 yards and rolled out of the end zone. Touchback.

The halftime score was 24-7, but in the last half, the Auburn defense held Alabama to 67 yards and only three points while the offense scored three touchdowns. The game winner came on a seven-yard throwback to tight end Philip Lutzenkirchen.

To win 28-27, all the Tigers did was pull off the biggest comeback in both Iron-Bowl and school history. No big deal.

Like the Iron Bowl, "big deals" are important components of the unfolding of our lives. Our wedding, childbirth, a new job, a new house, even a new car. In many ways, what we regard as a big deal is what shapes not only our lives but our character.

One of the most unfathomable anomalies of faith in America today is that while many people profess to be die-hard Christians, they disdain involvement with a local church. As Paul tells us, however, the Church is a very big deal to God; it is at the heart of his redemptive work; it is a vital part of his eternal purposes.

The Church is no accident of history. It isn't true that Jesus died and all he wound up with for his troubles was the stinking Church. It is no consolation prize.

Rather, the church is the primary instrument through which God's plan of cosmic and eternal salvation is worked out. And it doesn't get any bigger than that.

We know our offense can put up 24 points in a quarter, no problem.
-- Safety Zac Etheridge on why being behind Alabama was no big deal

**To disdain church involvement is to assert
that God doesn't know what he's doing.**

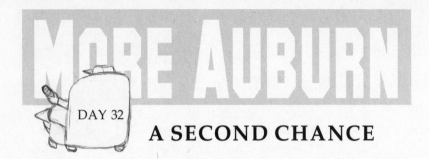

DAY 32

A SECOND CHANCE

Read John 7:53-8:11.

"'Then neither do I condemn you,' Jesus declared. 'Go now and leave your life of sin'" (v. 8:11).

Because Clemson got a second chance to tie the game, Auburn won it.

On Sept. 18, 2010, the 2-0 Tigers met the 2-0 Tigers at Jordan-Hare. Auburn was favored but promptly spent the whole first half being "alarmingly bad." The offense didn't even register a first down until eight minutes into the second quarter.

Meanwhile, the Tigers with the paws on their helmets were on the prowl, scoring the game's first seventeen points on their way to a 17-3 halftime lead.

Head coach Gene Chizik insisted no "magic" happened in the Auburn locker room at halftime. Just a few tweaks. Whatever happened in there, in the third quarter the hometown Tigers transformed themselves "from bumbling to brilliant."

They outgained Clemson by more than 200 yards and rolled up 21 points while shutting the visitors down. The venerable stadium was rocking and rolling, at one point players running to the student section to exhort the crowd to make even more noise.

But Clemson didn't fold, scoring in the fourth quarter to send the game into overtime at 24 each.

In the extra period, Wes Byrum kicked a 39-yard field goal for the Tigers, leaving Clemson a chance to win it with a touchdown.

TIGERS

The Auburn defense promptly bowed its collective backs and forced a field-goal try that sailed right through the uprights.

But the refs signalled a penalty on the play against Auburn that would give Clemson a first down close to the goal line. After the zebras huddled, though, they ruled the penalty was on Clemson. The center was guilty of double-clutching the snap.

Thus, Clemson had to tie the game a second time. Incredibly, the kick sailed wide left. Auburn had beaten the Tigers from the Palmetto State for the fourteenth straight time dating back to 1951.

"If I just had a second chance, I know I could make it work out." Ever said that? If only you could go back and tell your dad one last time you love him, take that job you passed up rather than relocate, or replace those angry shouts at your son with gentle encouragement. If only you had a second chance, a mulligan.

As the story of Jesus' encounter with the adulterous woman illustrates, with God you always get a second chance. No matter how many mistakes you make, God will never give up on you. Nothing you can do puts you beyond God's saving power. You always have a second chance because with God your future is not determined by your past or who you used to be. It is determined by your relationship with God through Jesus Christ.

God is ready and willing to give you a second chance – or a third chance or a fourth chance – if you will give him a chance.

I have to thank God for giving me the gift that he did as well as a second chance for a better life.
-- Olympic figure skating champion Oksana Baiul

**You get a second chance with God
if you give him a chance.**

DAY 33

TOP SECRET

Read Romans 2:1-16.

"This will take place on the day when God will judge men's secrets through Jesus Christ, as my gospel declares" (v. 16).

The Auburn coaches had such a red-hot secret on their hands that they hid it away at a hunting lodge and a movie theater. That secret was Tommy Lorino.

After the 1954 high-school football season, Lorino's dad put an end to the recruiting war that stretched all the way to Notre Dame by deciding his son would play for Auburn. At that time, alums could legally help with recruiting, and they worked closely with the coaches. With signing day nearing, the Auburn crew didn't want another school making a late run at their prized recruit. So they teamed Lorino up with running back Fob James, lineman Frank Reeves, and a few other Auburn players and spirited the whole bunch off to a hunting lodge near Eufaula.

It didn't matter that Lorino, raised a city boy, knew nothing about guns or hunting. What mattered was that he was out of sight for the three days leading up to signing day.

They then carted Lorino to a Birmingham hotel at 10 p.m. the night before signing day. There he met with the other Auburn recruits, and they were shuffled off to a movie. In the theater, they were all surrounded by a whole bunch of alums so nobody could get to them. Shortly before midnight, the recruits were ushered

TIGERS

back to the hotel, and at 12:01 a.m. the signing began.

All the secretive shenanigans evidently didn't hurt; three years later, the Tigers were national champions, and Lorino was a starting halfback on that team. An Auburn legend, he led the SEC in rushing all three seasons he played, setting a national record as a sophomore in 1956 by averaging 8.4 yards per carry. He also was the team's punter and starred on defense. He was inducted into the Alabama Sports Hall of Fame in 1999.

As Auburn once kept all recruiting news secret, so do we have to be vigilant about the personal information we prefer to keep secret. Much information about us -- from credit reports to what movies we rent -- is readily available to prying and persistent persons. In our information age, people we don't know may know a lot about us — or at least they can find out. And some of them may use this information for harm.

While diligence may allow us to be reasonably successful in keeping some secrets from the world at large, we should never deceive ourselves into believing we are keeping secrets from God. God knows everything about us, and that includes all the things we wouldn't want proclaimed at church. All our sins, mistakes, failures, shortcomings, quirks, prejudices, and desires – God knows all our would-be secrets.

But here's something God hasn't kept a secret: No matter what he knows about us, he loves us still.

It was like espionage, keeping us out of sight and hidden.
– Tommy Lorino on signing day

We have no secrets before God, and it's no secret
that he nevertheless loves us still.

DAY 34

PRAYER WARRIORS

Read Luke 18:1-8.

"Then Jesus told his disciples a parable to show them that they should always pray and not give up" (v. 1).

In the 2000 Auburn-Georgia game, the two old foes halted their combat long enough to engage in a remarkable act of sportsmanship: They prayed together for a fallen Auburn player.

Like so many of the contests in the Deep South's Oldest Rivalry, the 2000 game was a classic. The Tigers were ranked 22nd and were on their way to the championship of the SEC's West Division; the Dogs were ranked 14th.

Georgia led 13-3 at the half, but the Tigers rallied to force overtime at 23. Georgia kicked a field goal on its possession. Auburn responded with a touchdown drive, quarterback Ben Leard, a Georgia native, scoring from the 1 on a sneak for the 29-26 win.

Perhaps even more memorable than the dramatic finish, however, was what occurred in the second quarter. Auburn wide receiver Tim Carter caught a pass over the middle and was hit hard by a Georgia tackler. The blow was its strongest on Carter's head. When he stayed down, Jordan-Hare Stadium went quiet.

Medical personnel quickly ran to Carter, and the game was halted for fifteen minutes while he was tended to. Eventually, an ambulance drove onto the field and carried him away.

While the medical team worked with Carter, Auburn's players and coaches first gathered on their own and knelt in prayer. On the opposite side of the field, Georgia's players and coaches did the same. Then the two teams came together in one big huddle and prayed together for Carter's safety.

Their prayers were answered. He returned to the sideline later in the game.

Jesus taught his followers to do exactly what the Tigers and the Bulldogs did that November day: Always pray and never give up, never stop praying.

Any problems we may have with prayer and its results derive from our side, not God's. We pray for a while about something – perhaps fervently at first – but our enthusiasm wanes if we don't receive the answer we want exactly when we want it. Why waste our time by asking for the same thing over and over again?

But God's isn't deaf; God does hear our prayers and God does respond to them. As Jesus clearly taught, our prayers have an impact because they turn the power of Almighty God loose in this world. Thus, falling to our knees and praying to God is not a sign of weakness and helplessness. Rather, praying for someone or something is an aggressive act, an intentional ministry, a conscious and fervent effort on our part to change someone's life or the world for the better.

God responds to our prayers; we often just can't perceive or don't understand how he is working to make those prayers come about.

There are two things you can do with your head down: play golf and pray.
                                    -- World Golf Hall of Fame member Lee Trevino

Jesus taught us to always pray and never give up.

DAY 35

FAIL-SAFE

Read Luke 22:54-62.

"Peter remembered the word the Lord had spoken to him: 'Before the rooster crows today, you will disown me three times.' And he went outside and wept bitterly" (vv. 61b-62).

Demond Washington failed so miserably early on that Ole Miss decided to come at him again. He was glad of it and pulled off two huge plays that turned the game Auburn's way.

The 8-0 Tigers took on Ole Miss on Oct. 30, 2010, in the final leg of a tough four-game stretch. Sure enough, the 3-4 Rebels came out smoking, scoring the game's first touchdown. They trailed only 14-7 when they marched to the Auburn 29 and let fly with a long pass. Washington, a senior cornerback, apparently was in position to make a play. But he didn't.

The combination of a perfect pass and a diving grab by the Ole Miss receiver resulted in six points and "left the Auburn cornerback embarrassed. He pumped his arms in disgust. A failure is a failure and Washington was upset."

Washington had failed before. A transfer as a junior, he had demonstrated a distressing "penchant for assignment errors [that] made him an unreliable defender." In the 35-27 win over South Carolina on Sept. 25, though, the Tiger coaches saw something different from Washington. He had his first sack and nabbed his first interception, which led to a newfound confidence.

TIGERS

He needed it after the Ole Miss touchdown, but it showed up in his attitude. He wanted the Rebs to throw at him again. They quickly obliged him. Trailing 17-14 they recovered a fumble at the Auburn 18. Remembering that earlier touchdown, they threw right at Washington. This time he pulled down an interception.

After the score went to 24-17 in the second quarter, Washington made an even bigger special teams play, returning a kickoff 95 yards to blow the game wide open. Auburn won easily 51-31.

"I was happy they were picking on me," Washington said. As a writer put it: "Time from goat to hero: 10 minutes."

Failure is usually defined by expectations. A baseball player who hits .300 is a star, but he fails seventy percent of the time. We grumble about a postal system that manages to deliver billions of items without a hitch. We don't like Auburn to ever lose a game.

And we are often our own harshest critics, beating ourselves up for our failings because we expected better. Never mind that our expectations were unrealistic to begin with.

The bad news about life is that failure – unlike success -- is inevitable. Only one man walked this earth perfectly and we're not him. The good news about life, however, is that failure isn't permanent. In life, we always have time to reverse our failures as did Peter, he who failed our Lord so abjectly.

The same cannot be said of death. In death we eternally suffer the consequences of our failure to follow that one perfect man.

I had to redeem myself because I felt like I let the team down.
-- Demond Washington on recovering from his early failure vs. the Rebs

**Only one failure in life dooms us to eternal failure
in death: failing to follow Jesus Christ.**

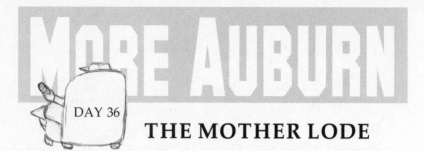

DAY 36

THE MOTHER LODE

Read John 19:25-30.

"Near the cross of Jesus stood his mother" (v. 25).

Nick Fairley's mother gave her son some tough advice instead of doing what he asked her to do -- and Auburn fans will forever be grateful.

In 2010, of course, Fairley, a junior defensive tackle, won the Lombardi Award as the top lineman in college football. As the defensive star of the national champions, he led the SEC with 10 1/2 sacks and 21 tackles for losses. Writer Lars Anderson called him "more unblockable than any defensive lineman in the nation."

Fairley played with a mean streak and earned a reputation for "his hard-charging, menacing style of play." After one game, his mother, Paula Rogers, called him up and asked him, "Why are you trying to hurt those quarterbacks." Fairley had to explain that he wasn't trying to hurt anyone, but "this is a man's game, and my job is to get that quarterback."

But Fairley always listened to his momma. After all, she gave him some stern advice once that changed the course of his life, and kept all his dreams alive though he didn't want to hear it.

Fairley committed to Auburn but did not qualify academically, so he enrolled in Copiah-Lincoln Community College in Wesson, Miss. He was redshirted in 2007 but started in 2008 and "immediately became Copiah-Lincoln's most dominating player." When the season ended, he recommitted to Auburn. The rest is Tiger legend and lore.

But had it all been up to Fairley, he might never have achieved any of that success, and Auburn may well not have won the 2010 national title. Only thirty minutes after his parents dropped him off in Wesson, he called his mother on her cell phone. "Mama, I want to come home," he pleaded.

She would have none of it. "I told him to hang in there and stay focused," Paula Rogers said. He did, and Nick Fairley's life and Auburn football were never the same.

Mamas often do the sort of thing Paula Rogers did for her son: offer tough advice though it may offer immediate pain and unhappiness. No mother in history, though, has faced a challenge to match that of Mary, whom God chose to be the mother of Jesus. Like mamas and their children throughout time, Mary experienced both joy and perplexity in her relationship with her son.

To the end, though, Mary stood by her boy. She followed him all the way to his execution, an act of love and bravery since Jesus was condemned as an enemy of the Roman Empire.

But just as mothers like Mary and Paula Rogers -- and perhaps yours -- would apparently do anything for their children, so will God do anything out of love for his children. After all, that was God on the cross at the foot of which Mary stood, and he was dying for you, one of his children.

The whole experience was eye opening. It changed his life.
— Paula Rogers on her son's taking her advice and staying in Wesson

**Mamas often sacrifice for their children,
but God, too, will do anything out of love
for his children, including dying on a cross.**

DAY 37

THE LONG HAUL

Read Luke 12:35-40.

"You also must be ready, because the Son of Man will come at an hour when you do not expect him" (v. 40).

The SEC football season is a long haul. If a team is to navigate it successfully, the players must adopt the attitude epitomized by the old "one-game-at-a-time" cliche. Few Auburn teams have done that better than did the 2004 Tigers.

The first hint that this squad had its collective head on straight came in the second week of the season. The Tigers opened up by rolling past Louisiana-Monroe 31-0. Next up was Mississippi State. The Bulldogs had a new head coach and had won only eight games in the last three seasons. They just didn't appear to be much of a threat. Moreover, dead ahead on the schedule for the Tigers was LSU, the defending national champions.

Thus, the encounter with the Bulldogs was a classic definition of a "trap game." "LSU is always in the back of your mind," admitted offensive tackle Marcus McNeil.

So how did the Tigers fare with their first chance to get caught looking ahead? Quite well, thank you.

Quarterback Jason Campbell threw three touchdown passes, two of them to wide receiver Anthony Mix, and the Tigers jumped out to a 21-0 halftime lead. They went on to cruise past State 43-14.

Ronnie Brown rushed for 147 yards and Carnell Williams had 123 as Auburn totally dominated the Bulldogs. "They beat us in about every way they could," said State head coach Sylvester Croom. State didn't cross the Auburn 30 in the first half, and the Dogs' two TDs didn't come until the last 83 seconds of the game.

Head coach Tommy Tuberville was relieved his team didn't overlook the Bulldogs. "With the intensity they played with today, it looked like they were focused on this game," he said.

The Tigers of 2004 were indeed in it for the long haul. They never got caught looking ahead and instead went undefeated and won the SEC championship.

Like a long football season with its share of road trips and tough games, life is an endurance sport; you're in it for the long haul. So you schedule a physical, check your blood pressure for free at the supermarket pharmacy, walk or jog, and hop on the treadmill that hides under the bed or doubles as a coat rack.

The length of your life, however, is really the short haul when compared to the long haul that is eternity. To prepare yourself for eternity requires conditioning that is spiritual rather than physical. Jesus prescribed a regimen so his followers could be in tip-top spiritual shape. It requires not just occasional exercise but a way of living every day that includes abiding faith, decency, witnessing, mercy, trust, and generosity.

If the Tigers aren't ready when the opposition kicks off, they lose a game. If you aren't ready when Jesus calls, you lose eternity.

We've been trying hard not to let them look ahead.
-- Auburn head coach Tommy Tuberville after the Miss. State game

Physical conditioning is good for the short run,
but you also need to be in peak spiritual shape
for the long haul.

DAY 38

HEAD GAMES

Read 1 Peter 1:3-14.

"Prepare your minds for action" (v. 13).

Celeste Troche was tough on the golf course, but the toughest part of her game wasn't physical but mental.

When she completed her collegiate career in 2003, Troche was "the most accomplished golfer in Auburn history, male or female." She was a four-time All-America and led the Tigers to two SEC championships (2000 and 2003) and a national runner-up finish in 2002. At the time, she had the six lowest 54-hole totals and the lowest stroke average for a season in Auburn history. She set the record (since broken) for most sub-par rounds in a season.

Troche started playing golf when she was 8. She was such a good golfer and such an outstanding student that her parents made a difficult but life-changing decision. She was raised in Paraguay, and her mom and dad decided to send her to the United States for her senior year of high school. She moved to Lanett, Ala., to live with relatives.

The change was tough. Troche spoke Spanish and German but not English. She was "in a strange, new world with a strange language and strange customs." She missed her family and she missed home. "I couldn't understand anything that was going on in class," she recalled. "I was getting ready to take the SAT and didn't even know what I was studying."

But she didn't cave in. Instead, she buckled down and demonstrated the mental toughness that helped carry her to success on the golf course. She worked hard, learned English, and became an outstanding student. She played on the boys' golf team in high school and said the challenge of being the only girl in the tournaments was "fun." "It would be 100 boys and me."

Celeste Troche was so mentally tough she turned challenges into fun.

Once upon a time, survival required mere brute strength, but persevering in American society today generally necessitates mental strength rather than physical prowess.

Your job, your family, your finances -- they all demand mental toughness from you by placing stress upon you to perform. Stress is a fact of life, though it isn't all bad as we are often led to believe. Stress can lead you to function at your best. Rather than buckling under it, you stand up, make constant decisions, and keep going.

So it is with your faith life. "Too blessed to be stressed" sounds nice, but followers of Jesus Christ know all about stress. Society screams compromise; your children whine about being cool; your company ignores ethics. But you don't fold beneath the stress; you keep your mind on Christ and the way he said to live because you are tough mentally, strengthened by your faith.

After all, you have the word and the grace of Almighty God for relief and support.

It was a good challenge and made me a better player. I had to work harder to beat the guys.
-- Celeste Troche on playing on the boys' golf team in high school

**Toughened mentally by your faith in Christ,
you live out what you believe, and you persevere.**

POP THE QUESTION

Read Matthew 16:13-17.

"'But what about you?' he asked. 'Who do you say I am?'" (v. 15)

At the midpoint of the 2010 season, fans and writers alike pondered the one great question surrounding the Auburn Tigers: "Why can't this team put four quarters together?" The Kentucky game sure didn't provide an answer.

In the first half on Oct. 9 in Lexington, the offense "made Kentucky defenders look silly and Auburn seemed on the verge of an attention-grabbing blowout." Cam Newton led the offense on four scoring drives of 78 yards or longer. Kentucky scored late to make it 31-17 at the break, but the Cats didn't appear to be a threat.

They were. The Auburn offense disappeared in the third quarter. About the same time, so did the defense. Kentucky tied it at 31, and then tied it again at 34 with 7:31 to play.

With the game and the season on the line, though, the offense returned to form -- not before flirting with disaster however. An attempted reverse on the kickoff was bobbled; Auburn recovered but back at its own 7. A few plays later, an end around resulted in a fumble that the refs reviewed and ruled had rolled out of bounds before Kentucky recovered it. Auburn's ball.

After that, what followed was Auburn lore. Newton led the Tigers on a 19-play, 82-yard drive that was a clock killer of epic proportions, using up 7 minutes and 22 seconds and ending at the

UK 11. As the clock ticked to zero, Wes Byrum calmly booted the fifth game-winning field goal of his career and his school-record 51st, breaking the old record of 50 set by John Vaughn. Kentucky never touched the ball again after tying the score at 34.

So the question remained: When would the Tigers put four quarters together? Apparently, it didn't seem to matter whether they ever did or not. All they did was win.

Life is an ongoing search for answers, and thus whether our life is lived richly or is wasted is largely determined by both the quality and the quantity of the answers we find. Life is indeed one question after another. What's for dinner? Can we afford a new car? What kind of team will Auburn have this season?

But we also continuously seek answers to questions at another, more crucial level. What will I do with my life? Why am I here? Why does God allow suffering and tragedy?

An aspect of wisdom is reconciling ourselves to and being comfortable with the fact that we will never know all of the answers. Equally wise is the realization that the answers to life's more momentous questions lie within us, not beyond us.

One question overrides all others, the one Jesus asked Peter: "Who do you say I am?" Peter gave the one and only correct answer: "You are the Son of the Living God." How you answer that question is really the only one that matters, since it decides not just how you spend your life but how you spend eternity.

We are finding interesting ways to end the games.
-- Gene Chizik on his team's tendency to play 'em close

**Only one question in life determines
your eternal fate: Who do you say Jesus is?**

DAY 40

REVELATION

Read Isaiah 53.

"But he was pierced for our transgressions, he was crushed for our iniquities; the punishment that brought us peace was upon him, and by his wounds we are healed" (v. 5).

Today was the first step toward winning the SEC championship." With that declaration, Auburn running back Lionel James revealed himself to be something of a prophet.

Head coach Pat Dye put his 1-1 Tigers through a rough week in preparation for the SEC opener in Knoxville on Sept. 24, 1983. The team scrimmaged Monday, Tuesday, and Wednesday. "We got a lot of folks hurt, but we weren't gonna come to Tennessee and get into a fight-for-your-life situation," Dye said.

And they didn't. The Tigers' wishbone offense, led by sophomore tailback Bo Jackson, controlled the line of scrimmage and the clock. Auburn held the ball for nearly a whole quarter longer than did the Volunteers, taking the crowd out of the game.

Auburn never trailed, but Tennessee was still hanging around at 19-7 until early in the fourth quarter. That's when true freshman Trey Gainous fielded a Volunteer punt at his own 19, cut up the middle, broke four tackles, and then used a final block from Jimmie Warren to finish off an 81-yard touchdown run.

After that, the Tigers romped to a 37-14 win. That 23-point margin matched the most Auburn had ever beaten Tennessee by.

TIGERS

In the locker room after the game, "Little Train" James, a senior, made his prediction. It came true. The '83 Tigers posted a 6-0 record in the SEC on their way to an 11-1 overall record and a win over Michigan in the Sugar Bowl.

What James didn't predict was a national championship, which that '83 squad can legitimately lay claim to. *The New York Times* voted the Tigers No. 1 in the country in its final poll.

In our jaded age, we have pretty much relegated prophecy to dark rooms in which mysterious women peer into crystal balls or clasp our sweaty palms while uttering some vague generalities. At best, we understand a prophet as someone who predicts future events as Lionel James did.

Within the pages of the Bible, though, we encounter something radically different. A prophet is a messenger from God, one who relays divine revelation to others.

Prophets seem somewhat foreign to us because in one very real sense the age of prophecy is over. In the name of Jesus, we have access to God through our prayers and through scripture. In searching for God's will for our lives, we seek divine revelation. We may speak only for ourselves and not for the greater body of Christ, but we do not need a prophet to discern what God would have us do. We need faith in the one whose birth, life, and death fulfilled more than 300 Bible prophecies.

I gave up a long time ago trying to predict the future and trying to deal with things I couldn't deal with.
-- Brett Favre

**Persons of faith continuously seek
a word from God for their lives.**

PROMISES, PROMISES

Read 2 Corinthians 1:16-20.

"No matter how many promises God has made, they are 'Yes' in Christ" (v. 20).

Gene Chizik kept a promise he made to his team -- just not when he said he would.

Prior to the 2011 Chick-fil-A bowl, Chizik promised his team they would attempt an onside kick after their first touchdown. That took a while as the Tigers couldn't move the ball on their first two possessions while the Virginia Cavaliers took a 7-0 lead.

The first big play of the night for Auburn came from Garrett Harper, a freshman walk-on wide-out. He broke through to block a Virginia punt. That set up a 3-yard touchdown run by freshman quarterback Kiehl Frazier and the tying extra point from another rookie, Cody Parkey.

The time had come for the head coach to keep his promise -- but he didn't. Instead, when the offense scored, he was busy with the defense. "I forgot," Chizik admitted.

He got another chance after Virginia took a 14-7 lead in the second quarter. Junior Barrett Trotter stepped in when starting quarterback Clint Moseley suffered an ankle injury, and on his second possession, he led the Tigers to a touchdown. The key play was a pass to wideout Emory Blake down to the 5-yard line. Tailback Onterio McCalebb then scored from the 3.

So what about that promise now, coach? This time, the assistants jogged Chizik's memory. Everyone was eager to try the on-side kick because the team had prepared for it. The head Tiger kept his promise. Parkey executed it flawlessly, "tapping the ball, following it and then waiting until it had rolled 10 yards before pouncing on it."

That play -- the result of a promise kept -- turned the game Auburn's way for good. Two plays later, Trotter hit Blake with a 50-yard bomb; Frazier then scored his second TD for a 21-14 Auburn lead. The Tigers were never headed and won easily 43-24.

The promises you make don't say much about you; the promises you keep tell everything.

The promise to your daughter to be there for her softball game. To your son to help him with his math homework. To your parents to come see them soon. To your spouse to remain faithful until death parts you. And remember what you promised God?

You may carelessly throw promises around, but you can never outpromise God, who is downright profligate with his promises. For instance, he has promised to love you always, to forgive you no matter what you do, and to prepare a place for you with him in Heaven.

And there's more good news in that God operates on this simple premise: Promises made are promises kept. You can rely absolutely on God's promises. The people to whom you make them should be able to rely just as surely on your promises.

I think we're undefeated on that onside kick.
-- Gene Chizik on the play that fulfilled a promise he'd made

God keeps his promises just as those
who rely on you expect you to keep yours.

DAY 42

UNBELIEVABLE!

Read Hebrews 3:7-19.

"See to it, brothers, that none of you has a sinful, unbelieving heart that turns away from the living God" (v. 12).

The whole 2010 football season was an unbelievable ride for Auburn fans. The most unbelievable play of the season, though, blew open the SEC title game.

As writer Andy Staples put it, "Auburn's perfect record belied a season of gritty, grinding comebacks." Everyone expected more of the same in the title game against 19th-ranked South Carolina. But the Tigers broke open a 7-7 tie with a 5-yard touchdown run by Cam Newton and a 54-yard TD pass from Newton to junior wide receiver Darvin Adams Thus, with a 21-7 lead after the first quarter in Atlanta on Dec. 4, "it seemed as if [Auburn] had finally been granted some breathing room."

Not yet, though. The Gamecocks proceeded to put together a drive that culminated in a touchdown with 16 seconds to play in the half. Auburn led 21-14, and the game gave all appearances of yielding up another "gritty, grinding" last half in the Tigers' drive for the BCS championship game.

Then came the most unbelievable play of the season.

On the final play of the first half, to no one's surprise, Newton let fly with a Hail Mary pass from the Auburn 49. Also to no one's surprise, South Carolina had it well covered. In fact, a Gamecock defender was the first player in the scrum to get his hands on the ball two yards into the end zone.

But the ball bounced off his hands into the mitts of a leaping Adams for a touchdown. In that unbelievable moment, the outcome of the game was decided. South Carolina was history.

The Tigers romped to a 28-3 advantage in the last half and won going away 56-17. The SEC championship was theirs.

Much of what taxes the limits of our belief system has little effect on our lives. Maybe we don't believe in UFOs, honest politicians, aluminum baseball bats, Sasquatch, or the viability of electric cars. A healthy dose of skepticism is a natural defense mechanism that helps protect us in a world that all too often has designs on taking advantage of us.

That's not the case, however, when Jesus and God are part of the mix. Quite unbelievably, we often hear people blithely assert they don't believe in God. Or brazenly declare they believe in God but don't believe Jesus was anything but a good man and a great teacher.

At this point, unbelief becomes dangerous because God doesn't fool around with scoffers. He locks them out of the Promised Land, which isn't a country in the Middle East but Heaven itself.

Given that scenario, it's downright unbelievable that anyone would not believe.

We've been in that situation in practice before, and repetition is the key to success.
-- Cam Newton on the unbelievable Hail Mary touchdown

Perhaps nothing is as unbelievable as that some people insist on not believing in God or his son.

DAY 43

REST EASY

Read Hebrews 4:1-11.

"There remains, then, a Sabbath rest for the people of God; for anyone who enters God's rest also rests from his own work, just as God did from his. Let us, therefore, make every effort to enter that rest" (vv. 9-11).

After giving its fans heart palpitations for three straight weeks," Auburn finally allowed them to rest easy for the afternoon.

On Sept. 9, 2010, the Tiger defense came to the rescue and held off Mississippi State 17-14. On the 18th, Auburn and Clemson went into overtime before the Carolina team missed a field goal, allowing Auburn to escape with a 27-24 win. The next weekend, Auburn trailed South Carolina in the fourth quarter before winning 35-27. In the last minute, the Gamecocks were throwing into the end zone.

As writer Bill Bryant put it, "It's hard to keep from watching," the come-from-behind Tigers. The thrilling, nail-biting finishes had gotten to the point that head coach Gene Chizik had no explanation for them except to say "it's a God thing."

So everybody -- the fans included -- needed a little break on a Saturday afternoon. They got it on Oct. 10 when the LA Monroe Warhawks flew into town.

The visitors were overmatched from the start. On the second play of the game, Onterio McCalebb busted a 50-yard TD run. Later in the quarter, Cam Newton spotted a wide-open Emory

Blake and hit him with a 94-yard touchdown pass.

By halftime, the 10th-ranked Tigers led 31-3 on their way to a 52-3 blowout. The coaches found sixty-eight bodies to put into the game. The second team took over in the third quarter; the third team mopped up in the fourth. Chizik admitted he gave his players as much rest as he could; the coaches didn't call a single running play for Newton, who was averaging 19 carries a game.

This day, prudence meant both players and fans got a welcome break from the tension and intensity of close games.

As part of the natural rhythm of life, rest is important to maintain physical health. Rest has different images, though: a good eight hours in the sack; a Saturday morning that begins in the backyard with the paper and a pot of coffee; a vacation in the mountains, where the most strenuous thing you do is change position in the hot tub.

Rest is also part of the rhythm and the health of our spiritual lives. Often we envision the faithful person as always busy, always doing something for God whether it's teaching Sunday school or showing up at church every time the doors open.

But God himself rested from work, and in blessing us with the Sabbath, he calls us into a time of rest. To rest by simply spending time in the presence of God is to receive spiritual revitalization and rejuvenation. Sleep refreshes your body and your mind; God's rest refreshes your soul.

Our plan was to keep [Cam Newton] from running too much.
-- Gus Malzahn on resting his quarterback some against ULM

God promises you a spiritual rest
that renews and refreshes your soul.

DAY 44

SOMETHING NEW

Read Colossians 3:1-17.

"[S]ince you have taken off your old self with its practices and have put on the new self, which is being renewed in knowledge in the image of its Creator" (vv. 9-10).

Why not try something new? Like a field goal when your team's undefeated and you've never even tried one before.

The Tigers of 1957 had upset Tennessee 7-0, romped past Chattanooga 40-7, and nudged Kentucky 6-0 when they arrived in Atlanta on Oct. 19 for a game against Georgia Tech. They were ranked in the top 10 and were leading the nation in total defense as they would for the season. The Tigers would also finish No. 1 in rushing defense, allowing only 67.4 yards per game.

Twice, Tech "rumbled ominously to the brink of the Auburn goal." The Jackets first made it to the four but disdained a field goal; a fourth-down pass fell incomplete in the end zone.

Tech's second threat was the more dangerous because it came in the fourth quarter. From the five, though, team captain Jimmy "Red" Phillips showed the world why he was an All-American defensive end that season. He crushed the Tech quarterback and forced a fumble that Lloyd Nix recovered.

The country's best collegiate defense gave up only 150 yards to Tech that afternoon, but Tech's defense was just as stingy. Nix was the game's top rusher with a paltry 48 yards on 13 carries.

Perhaps realizing how the game would go, Auburn head coach

TIGERS

Shug Jordan decided to try something new in the second quarter. Though the team did not have one yet that season, he called for a 31-yard field goal. Moreover, he let fullback Billy Atkins try it though he had never made one. In this season of destiny, Atkins' kick was good, and the three points stood up for the 3-0 win. He was mobbed after the game by his teammates.

"I was confident that it was going in there when I let the kick go," Atkins said. "I knew Billy could do it," declared Jordan, "but I couldn't say I was confident until I saw it going through there."

New things in our lives often have a life-changing effect. A new spouse. A new baby. A new job. Even something as mundane as a new television set or lawn mower jolts us with change.

While new experiences, new people, and new toys may make our lives new, they can't make new lives for us. Inside, where it counts – down in the deepest recesses of our soul – we're still the same, no matter how desperately we may wish to change.

An inner restlessness drives us to seek escape from a life that is a monotonous routine. Such a mundane existence just isn't good enough for someone who is a child of God; it can't even be called living. We want more out of life; something's got to change.

The only hope for a new life lies in becoming a brand new man or woman. And that is possible only through Jesus Christ, he who can make all things new again.

It was the first one I have ever made, and it couldn't have come at a better time.
-- Billy Atkins on his game-winning kick vs. Ga. Tech

A brand new you with the promise of a life worth living is waiting in Jesus Christ.

LET'S TALK ABOUT IT

Read Luke 24:13-35.

"Then the two told what had happened on the way" (v. 35).

This is one they'll be talking about another 75 years from now."

Everybody was certainly talking after Auburn rallied from 24 points down to edge Alabama 28-27 in the 2010 Iron Bowl. "This is probably the best game ever played in the history of Auburn," gushed linebacker Josh Bynes, who made ten tackles in the game "and set an NCAA record for hyperbole." "I don't think that's been done in history," he said about the Auburn comeback. "It's maybe been centuries." "The Iron Bowl is bigger than a national championship, really," proclaimed safety Zac Etheridge. Head coach Gene Chizik was considerably more subdued, but even he said the game was one "that will certainly go down in history."

Trailing 24-7 at the break, the Tigers did some talking in the locker room at halftime, but Cam Newton put an end to all the chitchat when he said, "Don't talk about what you're going to do. Just go out and do it."

The Tigers certainly went out and gave their fans something to talk about with the comeback that ultimately propelled the team to the national championship. Perhaps the play that will remain the most talked about through the years was one in the first half that just shouldn't have happened. Alabama led 21-0 when Heisman-Trophy winner Mark Ingram broke into the clear and headed for the end zone. Antoine Carter, a 256-pound defensive end, incredibly ran Ingram down from behind and knocked the ball loose. The result was a touchback instead of a touchdown.

"I really didn't [think I could catch Ingram]," Carter said about the play. "I just kept running. When you finish plays, great things happen."

On that day, great plays did happen that ultimately gave Auburn fans something to talk about – for a long, long, time.

Wins over Alabama and the players who make the key plays are indeed remembered and recalled whenever the Auburn faithful get together and talk football – which is all the time. Folks can't help themselves; they've just got to talk about these guys.

A similar situation occurred way back on that first Easter when a trio of travelers was hiking down the road. One wanderer must not have been from around there, so two of them had to tell him all about what had been going on. Then when the two men realized their companion was the risen Lord, they went to Jerusalem to talk some more, to tell others what had happened. They found another group as excited as they were and talking about the events of the day.

So it continues today; for almost two millennia now, people have talked about Jesus. That's because even today, just as it was for the two men on the road to Emmaus, meeting Jesus always leaves us with something to talk about.

It makes me feel fast.
-- Antoine Carter talking about catching Mark Ingram from behind

An encounter with the living Jesus
always leaves us with something to talk about.

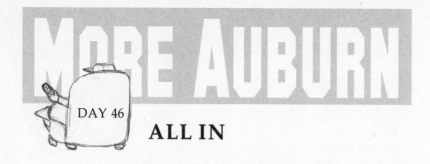

DAY 46

ALL IN

Read Mark 12:28-34.

"Love the Lord your God with all your heart and with all your soul and with all your mind and with all your strength" (v. 30).

In pregame warmups, the Auburn offense could barely contain its excitement and enthusiasm about a new trick play. The only problem was that the thing hadn't worked at all in practice.

On Oct. 16, 2004, the undefeated Tigers on their way to the SEC title welcomed the Arkansas Razorbacks to town. The coaches decided they needed to strike quickly to get Arkansas down early, so they devised a trick play and set about practicing it all week.

And how did it turn out? Well . . . "It worked sometime, but not as much as we wanted it to," claimed wide receiver Devin Aromashodu. Fellow receiver Courtney Taylor had an entirely different take on the play. "We only ran it successfully once," he said, "and Devin dropped it."

Nevertheless, the play was to be called during the first Auburn offensive series. "I didn't sleep [the night before the game]," Aromashodu said. "I was thinking about it the whole time."

Anticipation and enthusiasm about the play continued right on through the warmups. "Our managers and trainers kept asking if we were going to run it," said quarterback Jason Campbell. Well, they did. After the Tigers made a first down on their first two plays, offensive coordinator Al Borges "pulled the trigger." "The guys were so excited to run this play, and I just wanted to keep from overthrowing Devin [Aromashodu]," Campbell said.

Arkansas' defense was pulled in tight against the run, the perfect setup for the play. Campbell pitched the ball to tailback Carnell Williams, who ran left and handed the ball to Taylor, who was moving to his right. He tossed the ball back to Campbell, who lofted a strike to a wide-open Aromashodu down the sideline.

Only 1:10 into the game, the Tigers had a 67-yard touchdown pass and a 7-0 lead. All fired up, they rolled to a 38-20 win.

What fills your life, your heart, and your soul so much that you sometimes just can't help what you do? We all have zeal and enthusiasm for something, whether it's Auburn football, sports cars, our family, scuba diving, or stamp collecting.

But do we have a zeal for the Lord? We may well jump up and down, scream, holler, even cry – generally making a spectacle of ourselves – when Auburn scores. Yet on Sunday morning, if we go to church at all, we probably sit there showing about as much enthusiasm as we would for a root canal.

Of all the divine rules, regulations, and commandments we find in the Bible, Jesus made it crystal clear which one is number one: We are to love God with everything we have. All our heart, all our soul, all our mind, all our strength.

If we do that, our zeal and enthusiasm will burst forth. We just won't be able to help ourselves.

I was just hoping and praying it would work.
-- Devin Aromashodu on the trick play against Arkansas

The enthusiasm with which we worship God
reveals the depth of our relationship with him.

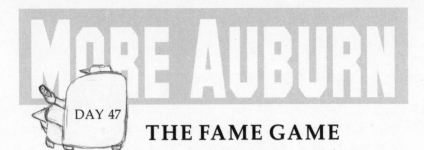

DAY 47

THE FAME GAME

Read 1 Kings 10:1-10, 18-29.

"King Solomon was greater in riches and wisdom than all the other kings of the earth. The whole world sought audience with Solomon" (vv. 23-24).

Lee Ziemba was just tagging along with a buddy to watch him receive an award. He had no idea he was "rock-star" famous.

In 2010, Ziemba was an All-American tackle and winner of the Jacobs Blocking Trophy as the SEC's best blocker. Center Ryan Pugh, who started 41 straight games, was first-team All-SEC and third-team All-America for the national champions.

On Feb. 8, 2011, the Montgomery Quarterback Club honored Pugh as its College Player of the Year. Ziemba said he was just hanging out before deciding at the last minute to ride along with his fellow lineman to watch him receive his trophy.

With Pugh as the honoree and team chaplain Chette Williams as the guest speaker, Ziemba probably expected he'd just get a free meal out of the deal, support his buddy, and stay in the background. Instead, he discovered he was as famous as a rock star.

As soon as the two linemen walked into the country club, they were swamped by excited Auburn fans. For more than an hour, they patiently posed for photographs and signed autographs. TV cameras rolled and eager fans shouted their names.

Pugh had already noticed how winning the title brought a measure of fame with it. "You go to these all-star games and

NFL workouts," he said, "and other players come up to you and they know you because you played in the national championship game and they watched you."

At least that night in Montgomery, Pugh and Ziemba didn't seem to mind the hullabaloo one bit. They both wore big smiles the whole time.

Have you ever wanted to be famous? Hanging out with other rich and famous people, having folks with microphones listen to what you say, throwing money around like toilet paper, meeting adoring and clamoring fans, signing autographs, and posing for the paparazzi before you climb into your imported sports car?

Many of us yearn to be famous, well-known in the places and by the people that we believe matter. That's all fame amounts to: strangers knowing your name and your face.

The truth is that you are already famous where it really does matter, which excludes TV's talking heads, screaming teenagers, rapt moviegoers, or D.C. power brokers. You are famous because Almighty God knows your name, your face, and everything else there is to know about you.

If a persistent photographer snapped you pondering this fame – the only kind that has eternal significance – would the picture show the world unbridled joy or the shell-shocked expression of a mug shot?

It's sinking in more and more every day.
  – Lee Ziemba on the fame that came with winning the national title

**You're already famous because
God knows your name and your face,
which may be either reassuring or terrifying.**

HEART OF THE MATTER

Read Matthew 6:19-24.

*"Store up for yourselves treasures in heaven . . . . For
where your treasure is, there your heart will be also" (vv.
20, 21).*

Alabama got $2 but Auburn got David Housel's heart.

In January 2005, Housel retired as Auburn's athletic director
after eleven seasons on the job. Prior to that, he was the athletic
department's sports information director. He dedicated more
than forty years to the university. In October of 2005, the press
box at Jordan-Hare Stadium was named for him.

With his decades of close association with AU football, Housel
was in a unique position following the 2010 season to compare that
team to the 1957 national champions. His assessment? There's no
comparison. "The 2010 team was a far better football team overall," Housel said. "But the 1957 team was the best team of its day."
Housel said comparing the two teams was "like comparing home
run champions from different eras. It's a different game now."

The 2010 team "was faster, bigger and stronger and had a great
offense," Housel said. That '57 team, which beat Alabama 40-0,
"had a dull, slow offense, but the defense would knock you on
your can. That's how the game was played then."

Housel became an Auburn fan in 1956, and little more than a
year later, he experienced the exultation and joy of that national
title. Fifty-five years later, in the aftermath of the win over Oregon,

TIGERS

he recalled the many fans he knew who didn't live to see the 2010 title. "I was one of the blessed ones, one of the lucky ones, who got to see it," he said.

But he didn't start out an Auburn fan. He grew up in Gordo, which is much closer to Alabama than Auburn. After his dad took him to the 1956 Iron Bowl, which Auburn won 34-7, he wrote letters to both schools. "Auburn sent me a media guide and a note thanking me for my interest in Auburn. Alabama sent me a media guide and a bill for $2," Housel recounted.

From that day on, Auburn had Housel's heart. Alabama had $2.

We often face decisions in life that force us to choose between our heart and our head. Our head says take that job with the salary increase; our heart says don't relocate because the kids are doing so well. Our head declares now is not the time to start a relationship; our heart insists that we're in love.

We wrestle with our head and our heart as we determine what matters the most to us. When it comes to the ultimate priority in our lives, though, our head and our heart tell us it's Jesus.

What that means for our lives is a resolution of the conflict we face daily: That of choosing between the values of our culture and a life of trust in and obedience to God. The two may occasionally be compatible, but when they're not, our head tells us what Jesus wants us to do; our heart tells us how right it is that we do it.

If it's something that you really want to do in your heart, stick with it and work hard and just keep your faith in Christ.
-- All-Pro defensive back Ty Law

**In our struggle with competing value systems,
our head and our heart lead us to follow Jesus.**

DAY 49

GIFT-WRAPPED

Read James 1:13-18.

"Every good and perfect gift is from above, coming down from the Father of the heavenly lights" (v. 17).

An Auburn football team once threatened to go on strike -- unless they received the gifts they had been promised.

The Tigers of 1953 went 7-2-1. A win over Alabama meant the SEC title and a berth in the Cotton Bowl, but the Tide won 10-7, relegating Auburn to the Gator Bowl.

A trip to Jacksonville didn't impress the Auburn players one bit. "We were not happy about it," said senior quarterback and team captain Vince Dooley. The players just didn't want to play much of anywhere after the disappointing loss to Alabama. "We were all down," Dooley admitted. But the players agreed to play after the coaches told them the bowl had promised to give them each watches and jackets.

The bowl bid meant the players had to practice over the holidays, and one day they tried to psych themselves up for the trip by talking about the nice watches and jackets they would be getting. An assistant coach then dropped a bombshell, telling them they weren't going to get anything at all. "You're going to play the game and that's it," he barked.

Well, it wasn't. The players got together that night and voted to strike. They were all for leaving campus right then until Dooley talked them into letting him meet with head coach Shug Jordan the next morning before they packed up.

When the two met, Jordan explained that he had made the promise in good faith, relying on what bowl officials had told him. He then met with the team at practice that afternoon and explained the mix-up. The players didn't say a word.

Two days later, Jordan told them he had just gotten word they would all receive their watches and jackets.

Receiving a gift is nice, but giving has its pleasures too, doesn't it? The children's excitement on Christmas morning. That smile of pure delight on your spouse's face when you came up with a really cool anniversary present. Your dad's surprise that time you didn't give him a tie or socks. There really does seem to be something to this being more blessed to give than to receive.

No matter how generous we may be, though, we are grumbling misers compared to God, who is the greatest gift-giver of all. That's because all the good things in our lives – every one of them – come from God. Friends, love, health, family, the air we breathe, the sun that warms us, even our very lives are all gifts from a profligate God. And here's the kicker: He even gives us eternal life with him through the gift of his son.

What in the world can we possibly give God in return? Our love and our life.

From what we get, we can make a living; what we give, however, makes a life.

– Arthur Ashe

**Nobody can match God when it comes to giving,
but you can give him the gift
of your love in appreciation.**

DAY 50

THE BIG TIME

Read Matthew 2:19-23.

"He went and lived in a town called Nazareth" (v. 23).

This is the big time, guys." As it turned out, it wasn't at all for the man who spoke those words.

Sitting high in the stands at War Memorial Stadium in Little Rock, a 29-year-old high-school football coach whose team would play for the 1994 state championship the next day delivered that pronouncement to his players. The coach was Gus Malzahn, who had no idea he would find his way to the real big time.

"It was a little overwhelming," Malzahn said of his team's appearance in those '94 finals. It certainly was a big deal for the tiny town of Hughes, Ark., that today has only about 2,000 inhabitants. The head coach figured the 1994 championship game was about his only chance to hit the big time, so he'd better not blow it.

Malzahn certainly wasn't in the big time at Hughes. He lived in a trailer with his wife and two daughters. He taught geography to seventh graders and health to high-school kids. After he was promoted to the head job in 1991, he bought a book to teach himself the game. "I didn't have a clue what I was doing," he said.

Malzahn may have been young and inexperienced, but he was smart and confident. Immediately, he turned his team into an offensive laboratory. "He was always doodling," said his athletic director at the time.

Hughes lost that '94 title game 17-13. "I thought I'd never be back," he recalled. "I thought I'd never get a chance again." But he did, eventually helping Auburn to the national championship in 2010 as the offensive coordinator. Malzahn had hit the big time, directing an offense that, interestingly enough, ran a scheme nearly identical to what that Hughes team did in 1994.

"It's the opposite end of the spectrum," Malzahn said about his time at Auburn. "I'm a high school coach who just happened to be coaching college." At the highest level of them all.

Like Gus Malzahn, the move to the big time is one we often desire to make in our own lives. Bumps in the road, one-stoplight communities, and towns with only convenience store, a church, and a voting place litter the American countryside.

Maybe you were born in one of them and grew up in a virtually unknown village in a backwater county. Perhaps you started out on a stage far removed from the bright lights of Broadway, the glitz of Hollywood, or the halls of power in Washington, D.C.

Those original circumstances don't have to define or limit you, though, for life is more than geography. It is about character and walking with God whether you're in the countryside or the city.

Jesus certainly knew the truth of that. After all, he grew up in a small town in an inconsequential region of an insignificant country ruled by foreign invaders.

Where you are doesn't matter. What you are does.

God's been so good to me, and I don't know why.
-- Gus Malzahn on his big-time coaching career

Where you live may largely be the culmination
of a series of circumstances;
what you are is a choice you make.

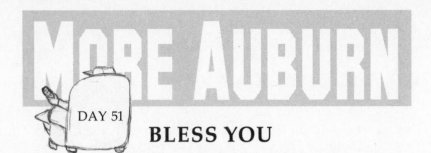

BLESS YOU

Read Romans 5:1-11.

"We also rejoice in our sufferings because we know that suffering produces perseverance; perseverance, character; and character, hope. And hope does not disappoint us"
(vv. 3-5a).

He was never a star and never received a bunch of honors and awards. So what one word did Quindarius Carr use to describe his time at Auburn? "Blessed."

Carr wound up at Auburn via Germany and Montana. When his dad retired from the military, the family settled in Huntsville. He simply showed up one day to watch the high school football team practice and asked the coaches if he could play. He was soon considered one of the state's top recruits at wide receiver.

Carr came to Auburn in 2007 and was redshirted. He went on to experience what he called "rock bottom" because of the head coaching change with all its anxiety. On the other side, Carr went to the "top of the college football world" with its view of "sheer perfection" when the 2010 Tigers won the national title.

Through it all, Carr played in every Auburn game for four seasons, but he was never a star. In 2008, he caught six passes; he caught only two passes in 2009. The second one, though, was a 46-yard grab that went for a touchdown, his first, in the Outback Bowl. He also played some on special teams.

During the national championship season, Carr saw some

additional action as the main option on punt returns. He caught three passes, two for touchdowns. "I feel good about my season," he said. "I did everything I could to help my team win."

That attitude continued in 2011 when Carr caught eight more passes. "He's definitely been a leader for us out there," said fellow receiver Emory Blake. For his career, Carr snared 19 passes for 417 yards, not the stuff of wide-receiver stardom.

Nevertheless, Carr said, "I've had an awesome time at Auburn. "I got my degree. I made plenty of friends. I would never take this back. Ever. Coming to Auburn has been a blessing."

We just never know what God is up to. We can know, though, that he's always busy preparing blessings for us and that if we trust and obey him, he will pour out those blessings upon us.

Some of those blessings, however, come disguised as hardship and suffering. That's often true in our own lives, too, and it is only after we can look back upon what we have endured that we understand it as a blessing.

The key lies in trusting God, in realizing that God isn't out to destroy us but instead is interested only in doing good for us, even if that means allowing us to endure the consequences of a difficult lesson. God doesn't manage a candy store; more often, he relates to us as a stern but always loving father. If we truly love and trust God, no matter what our situation is now, he has blessings in store for us. This, above all, is our greatest hope.

Always have the attitude of gratitude and count your blessings.
-- Former NFL head coach Tony Dungy

Life's hardships are often transformed into blessings when we endure them trusting in God.

DAY 52

STORY TIME

Read Luke 8:26-39.

"'Return home and tell how much God has done for you.'
So the man went away and told all over town how much
Jesus had done for him" (v. 39).

The Auburn Tigers of 2004 were SEC champions, but they were also something much more important: They were witnesses for Jesus Christ.

On Wednesday night before the Tennessee game of Oct. 2, team chaplain Chette Williams asked sophomore tight end Kyle Derozan to sing at the weekly Fellowship of Christian Athletes meeting. He sang "this song I knew growing up," a hymn called "Hard Fighting Soldier."

Friday night in Knoxville, toward the end of the team's prayer time, Derozan sang the hymn again by request. This time, everyone joined in. "In an instant," Williams said, "the room transformed from a quiet chapel to a raucous gathering of praise and worship. We stood up and locked arms, swaying with the verses and singing loud enough for people to hear us in the lobby."

On Saturday, at the moment when the team ran onto the field, somebody shouted out, "Hey, let's hook up." The players locked arms, and instead of sprinting onto the field, "they walked with confidence -- not the cocky stride of players who know how good they are, but [with the] quiet confidence [from] knowing that God was ordering their steps." For the rest of the season, the players

TIGERS

sang "Hard Fighting Soldier" the night before the game and hooked up as they walked onto the field for the game.

Then in the locker room after the win over Ole Miss, with a 9-0 record and the championship of the SEC West locked up, the players sang again. The "locker room became the prayer room as players hooked up arm in arm and started singing and swaying and laughing in a thanksgiving spirit."

On his television show that week, head coach Tommy Tuberville showed that locker-room scene of the Tigers joyously witnessing for Jesus.

Like the Tigers of 2004, you have a story to tell; it's the story of your life and it's unique. No one else among the billions of people on this planet can tell the same story.

Part of that story is your encounter with Jesus. It's the most important chapter of all, but all too often the believers in Jesus Christ don't tell it. Otherwise brave and daring Christian men and women who wouldn't think twice of skydiving or whitewater rafting often quail when we are faced with the prospect of speaking about Jesus to someone else. It's the dreaded "W" word: witness. "I just don't know what to say," we sputter.

But witnessing is nothing but telling your story. No one can refute it; no one can claim it isn't true. You don't get into some great theological debate for which you're ill prepared. You just tell the beautiful, awesome story of Jesus and you.

God had transformed us into witnesses.
-- Chette Williams on the 2004 Tigers

We all have a story to tell, but the most important part of all is the chapter where we meet Jesus.

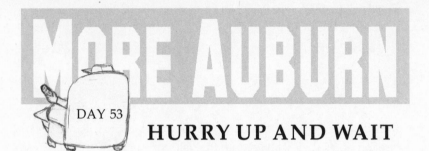

DAY 53

HURRY UP AND WAIT

Read Acts 1:1-14.

"Do not leave Jerusalem, but wait for the gift my Father promised, which you have heard me speak about" (v. 4).

Philip Lutzenkirchen sure got tired of waiting for his time to come. When it did, though, the wait was worth it.

Lutzenkirchen arrived in Auburn in 2009 as a big receiver with a lot of hype. He didn't expect to have to wait around to be a significant part of the offense -- but he did.

His freshman season, Lutzkirchen platooned at tight end and saw action in all thirteen games. He caught only five passes all year, though, two of which went for touchdowns. He pretty much disappeared from the offense late in the season, not catching a pass in the last three games.

Lutzenkirchen expected to get the ball more in 2010, but the first three games went by without a single reception. Despite the waiting, he remained patient. "Everyone wants the ball more," he said after the win over Clemson that upped the Tigers' record to 3-0. "I'm not complaining. Whenever I get the ball, I'm going to do what I can with it."

He kept his promise when the waiting ended the following week in the win over South Carolina. Lutzenkirchen caught three passes, one for a touchdown. Wideout Emory Blake described the nab in the end zone as "a tough catch."

Lutkenkirchen was on his way to a record-setting career. He

finished the national championship season with fifteen catches for 185 yards and five touchdowns, which put him third on the team in TD receptions and fourth in yardage. In 2011, he had a team-high seven scoring catches and was second team All-SEC. With his senior season of 2012 still to go, he had already set the Auburn record for TD catches by a tight end with fourteen.

The wait -- especially for Auburn fans -- was well worth it.

You rush to your doctor's appointment and wind up sitting in the appropriately named waiting room for an hour. You wait in the concessions line at an Auburn game. You're put on hold when you call a tragically misnamed "customer service" center. All of that waiting is time in which we seem to do nothing but feel the precious minutes of our life ticking away.

Sometimes we even wait for God. We have needs, and we desperately call upon the Lord and are disappointed when we perhaps get no immediate answer.

But Jesus' last command to his disciples was to wait. Moreover, the entire of our Christian life is spent in an attitude of waiting for Jesus' return. While we wait for God, we hold steadfast to his promises, we continue our ministry, we remain in communion with him through prayer and devotion.

In other words, we don't just wait; we grow stronger in our faith. Waiting for God is never time lost.

I just had to be patient. I knew my time was coming to get some touches.
-- Philip Lutzenkirchen

Since God acts on his time and not ours,
we often must wait for him,
using the time to strengthen our faith.

DAY 54

FRIENDS FOREVER

Read Ecclesiastes 4:9-12.

"If one falls down, his friend can help him up. But pity the man who falls and has no one to help him up!" (v. 10)

They were the odd couple of SEC football, an Auburn safety and an Ole Miss running back who became friends because they collided violently during a game -- and one pretty much saved the other's life.

In Auburn's 33-20 win of Oct. 31, 2009, junior safety Zac Etheridge smashed into running back Rodney Scott with Tiger linebacker Eltoro Freeman also part of the collision. Freeman hopped up at once; Etheridge didn't because Scott lay across him. But Scott hesitated about getting up when he couldn't feel the Auburn player moving under him. "When he made no effort to get up, I just stayed as still as I could," Scott said.

The trainers hurried out; the Ole Miss back told them he wasn't injured, but when they asked Etheridge, he didn't reply though he was conscious. He couldn't move. All he could do was whisper a barely audible prayer while the Jordan-Hare crowd went silent and players from both teams knelt to pray. "I was in shock, so all I could say was 'Jesus, Jesus,'" Etheridge recalled. "I just kept calling His name over and over."

For ten minutes, Scott didn't move while the trainers strapped Etheridge to a backboard. The Auburn player was indeed seriously injured; he had torn neck ligaments and a fractured vertebra, injuries that ended his season but ultimately did not threaten his life or his career. Doctors called Scott a hero and told him that had he moved at all, Etheridge could well have been left paralyzed.

The two stayed in touch, two SEC warriors chatting and keeping up with each other, what may well be a lifelong friendship the unexpected result of a potential tragedy.

Etheridge returned in 2010 to start for the national champions, finishing as the team's second-leading tackler.

Lend him your car or some money. Provide tea, sympathy, and comfort him when she's down. Talk him out of a bad decision like attending Alabama. What wouldn't you do for a good friend?

We are wired for friendship. Our psyche drives us to seek both the superficial company of others that casual acquaintance provides and the more meaningful intimacy that true friendship furnishes. We are perhaps at our noblest when we selflessly help a friend.

So if we wouldn't think of turning our back on our friends, why would we not be the truest, most faithful friend of all by sharing with them the gospel of Jesus Christ? Without thinking, we give a friend a ride, but we know someone for years and don't do what we can to save her from eternal damnation. Apparently, we are quite willing to spend all of eternity separated from our friends. What kind of lousy friend is that?

It is kind of weird, but personally I need to stay in touch with the guy who basically saved my life.
-- Zac Etheridge on his friendship with Rodney Scott

**A true friend introduces a friend
to his friend Jesus.**

PROBLEM CHILD

Read Luke 7:18-39.

"But the Pharisees and experts in the law rejected God's purpose for themselves, because they had not been baptized by John" (v. 30).

Auburn head football coach Shug Jordan had a whole mess of problems on his hands as the season began.

Always in the background for the team was probation. The season before, the Tigers had received the stiffest penalty the NCAA had ever handed out. Thus, this particular season arrived with no promise of a bowl game, which presented some motivational problems for the coaches.

The schedule was no help. The Tigers opened the season on the road against Tennessee, which had finished at No. 2 in the nation the season before and was the pick to win the conference.

The offense also had some problems that revealed themselves in a sluggish 12-9 spring game. Halfback was in good shape with Tommy Lorino and Bobby Hoppe. Still, Jordan was so concerned about what he perceived as a punchless offensive attack that he sent coaches to Norman, Okla., to scout the Sooners.

Then came a really big problem. Jordan kicked both his starting quarterback and his starting fullback off the team for "academic and disciplinary" reasons. In announcing the dismissals to his dumbstruck team, Jordan said, "Gentlemen, down through the years, we here at Auburn have learned to live with adversity. But adversity, as we know, tends to draw men together."

To heck with adversity. Who was gonna play quarterback? Jordan solved that problem by moving halfback Lloyd Nix, who had thrown all of one pass the season before, into the spot.

That team evidently did a pretty good job of solving its problems. This was 1957, and they won the national championship.

Problems are such a ubiquitous feature of our lives that a whole day without a single problem ranks right up there with an Auburn team that never, ever loses a game and entertaining, wholesome television programs. We just can't even imagine it.

But that's life. Even Jesus had more than his share of problems with his followers, the religious establishment, and nonbelievers. He could have easily removed all problems from his daily walk, but what good would that have done us? Our goal is to become like Jesus, and we could never fashion ourselves after a man who didn't encounter job stress, criticism, loneliness, temptation, frustration, and discouragement.

Instead, Jesus showed us that when – not if – problems come, a person of faith uses them to get better rather than letting the problems use him to get bitter. We learn God-filled perseverance and patience as we develop and deepen our faith and our trust in God. Problems will pass; eternity will not.

Unless Coach Ralph 'Shug' Jordan can come up with a smart quarterback, his giant may be slow-footed and dim-witted.
  -- Sports Illustrated's '57 preseason take on the Tigers

**The problem with problems is that
we often let them use us and become bitter
rather than using them to become better.**

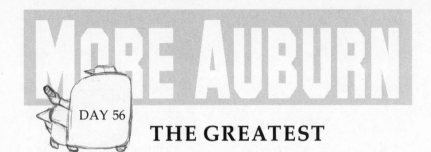

THE GREATEST

Read Mark 9:33-37.

"If anyone wants to be first, he must be the very last, and the servant of all" (v. 35).

Auburn believes it's on the cusp of something great." What unfolded was the greatest season in Auburn football history.

As the Tigers prepared for the 2010 season, a then-unknown quarterback named Cam Newton was peeved and didn't mind saying so. Yes, he was aware that other school in the state had won the national title the season before. He just couldn't figure out what that had to do with the way the media perceived Auburn's 2010 squad and why Alabama was getting all the hype. "We feel like we're not being mentioned as we should be," Newton said.

Certainly Auburn was an intriguing team as the 2010 season neared. After the disaster of 2008, they won eight games in 2009 under new coach Gene Chizik and set school records for points, yards, passing touchdowns, and number of plays. Unfortunately, they also set a school record for points allowed.

But 2010 was the second year for the defense under coordinator Ted Roof, and this year he had the luxury of depth. The Tigers added thirty new players since the win over Northwestern in the Outback Bowl. Eleven of them were linebackers and defensive backs. So in 2010, the defense was loaded with both experience and bodies. Four offensive-line starters, all three linebackers, experienced safeties and cornerbacks -- all returned.

TIGERS

The situation with the offense was much the same with nine starters who had extensive playing time returning. One of the newcomers was Newton. With all that experience -- especially in the line -- offensive coordinator Gus Malzahn believed the offense would be even better than it was in 2009.

So those who looked closely at the 2010 Tigers in August saw a team with no apparent weaknesses. As guard Bart Eddins put it, "The only real weaknesses [we have] are ones we create ourselves."

The Tigers stood poised for their greatest season ever.

We all want to be the greatest. The goal for the Tigers and their fans every season is the national championship. The competition at work is to be the most productive sales person on the staff or the Teacher of the Year. In other words, we define being the greatest in terms of the struggle for personal success. It's nothing new; Jesus' disciples saw greatness in the same way.

As Jesus illustrated, though, greatness in the Kingdom of God has nothing to do with the secular world's understanding of success. Rather, the greatest are those who channel their ambition toward the furtherance of Christ's kingdom through love and service, rather than their own advancement, which is a complete reversal of status and values as the world sees them.

After all, who could be greater than the person who has Jesus for a brother and God for a father? And that's every one of us.

I guess if you win games, you'll silence all the critics.
-- Cam Newton prior to the 2010 season

To be great for God has nothing to do with personal advancement and everything to do with the advancement of Christ's kingdom.

WEATHERPROOFED

Read Nahum 1:3-9.

"His way is in the whirlwind and the storm, and clouds are the dust of his feet" (v. 3b).

Auburn's preparations for the biggest game of the 2004 season (short of the Iron Bowl) were at the mercy of the weather.

Hurricane Ivan hit the Alabama coast the Thursday before the Sept. 18 game against the 4th-ranked LSU Tigers. Discussions as to whether the game should be played started early in the week with LSU seeking to postpone it. Auburn had no such intentions.

The uncertainty, though, forced some major changes in and severe inconveniences on the players and their preparation for the game against the defending national champions. The school cancelled classes and students ran for home. With the campus practically deserted, the team moved into a downtown hotel.

That was not a situation the players particularly liked since it gave the coaches constant access to them. "We had to meet something like 10 hours a day," lamented defensive end Bret Eddins. "It was all we could do because we were stuck in the hotel."

Even when they had free time, the players battled boredom. "There's nothing worse than just sitting around and the power was off and it was hot," Eddins said. (The coaches used generators to run the video equipment.) "It was a little scary, too, sitting there listening to the wind hit the windows."

The Tigers did make time for practice, but their workouts had

TIGERS

to be moved to their indoor facility. Since it included only half a field, only one unit could practice at a time.

Strength and conditioning coach Kevin Yoxall was aware of the exceptional situation. "Our preparation from a physical standpoint flew in the face of everything I've ever preached," he said.

The coaches were concerned and the players had cabin fever, but not even the weather could stop the Tigers. They won 10-9, taking a huge step toward the SEC championship.

A thunderstorm washes away your golf game or the picnic with the kids. Lightning knocks out the electricity just as you settle in at the computer. A tornado interrupts your Sunday dinner and sends everyone scurrying to the hallway. A hurricane blows away your beach trip or threatens a football game.

For all our technology and our knowledge, we are still at the mercy of the weather, able only to get a little more advance warning than in the past. The weather answers only to God. Rain and hail will fall where they want to, totally inconsiderate of something as important as an Auburn football game.

We stand mute before the awesome power of the weather, but we should be even more awestruck at the power of the one who controls it, a power beyond our imagining. Neither, however, can we imagine the depths of God's love for us, a love that drove him to die on a cross for us.

You can't control the weather, so we just have to know how to adjust.
-- Quarterback Jason Campbell on the week of the LSU game

The power of the one who controls the weather is
beyond anything we can imagine,
but so is his love for us.

DAY 58

A ROARING SUCCESS

Read Galatians 5:16-26.

"So I say, live by the Spirit. . . . The sinful nature desires what is contrary to the Spirit. . . . The acts of the sinful nature are obvious: . . . I warn you, as I did before, that those who live like this will not inherit the kingdom of God" (vv. 16, 17, 19, 21).

The Tigers needed some success on the field, and they needed it right away. They got it by dialing up a brand new play.

Though the Tigers had scored the half's last touchdown, no one had any doubts that they were in trouble at halftime of the 2010 Iron Bowl. Alabama led 24-7 and had the offensive edge 379 yards to 87. What could they do to be more successful?

That was the discussion in the Auburn locker room at halftime. The coaches had some answers. They tweaked the schemes on both sides of the ball; they changed the game plan a little bit. They carefully reviewed why Alabama had been so successful while they hadn't been able to do much.

Overall, the coaches and the players talked about what they had to do over the last two quarters. Specifically, everyone agreed they needed some success immediately. "We wanted [that opening drive of the second half] to be successful," said wideout Terrell Zachery. "We knew if we could get something good to happen and put some points on the board, we could keep it rolling."

Those points went up on the second play of that opening drive.

Offensive coordinator Gus Malzahn called a play that had been inserted into the playbook only the week before. It completely confused the Alabama secondary, and Zachery blew past them. Cam Newton hit him with a strike, and 70 yards later Auburn trailed only 24-13.

That early success keyed a comeback that will forever be a part of Auburn lore.

Are you a successful person? Your answer, of course, depends upon how you define success. Is the measure of your success based on the number of digits in your bank balance, the square footage of your house, that title on your office door, or the size of your boat?

Certainly the world determines success by wealth, fame, prestige, awards, and possessions. Our culture screams that life is all about gratifying your own needs and wants. If it feels good, do it. It's basically the Beach Boys' philosophy of life.

But all success of this type has one glaring shortcoming: You can't take it with you. Eventually, Daddy takes the T-bird away. Like life itself, all these things are fleeting.

A more lasting and valid approach to success is through the spiritual rather than the physical. The goal becomes not money or back-slaps by sycophants but eternal life spent with God. Success of that kind is forever.

That was a big thing we talked about -- having early success.
-- Terrell Zachery on turning the Iron Bowl around

Success isn't permanent, and failure isn't fatal
-- unless you're talking about
your relationship with God.

DAY 59

DON'T STOP NOW

Read 1 Thessalonians 5:12-22.

"Be joyful always; pray continually; give thanks in all circumstances, for this is God's will for you in Jesus Christ" (vv. 16-18).

The Tigers never stopped hustling all season, not even when it looked as though the play were over. In the biggest game of them all, it made all the difference in the world.

In the BCS championship game of Jan. 10, 2011, the Oregon Ducks scored with 2:33 left to forge a tie at 19. All they needed was a stop – or as *Sports Illustrated* put it, "one lousy stop" – to force overtime and win it with their explosive offense. Cam Newton hit sophomore wide receiver Emory Blake for a 15-yard gain, but then the Ducks looked like they had a stop in the making. Instead, what happened was "a sequence more surreal than the lime-green Day-Glo stockings that Oregon's marketing gurus unveiled for the occasion."

True freshman running back Michael Dyer took a handoff from Newton and was thrown to the ground by an Oregon defender. "Play came to a stop. The Ducks' defense relaxed." Dyer himself popped up and stopped – only to hear his coaches and some teammates screaming "Run!" and "Go!"

So Dyer did, taking off down the right sideline for a 37-yard gain. What the frantic coaches and some players had seen was that Dyer had rolled over the defender instead of touching the ground, his right knee and leg grazing the grass and not hitting the turf. "At the time I wasn't really sure I was down," Dyer said. "I was sort of waiting to hear a whistle." But there was no whistle.

A lengthy review followed, the result of which was to confirm that a whole bunch of Tigers had really good eyesight; the play was allowed to stand. Five plays later, Wes Byrum booted the game-winning field goal that Michael Dyer's refusal to stop had turned into a chip shot.

Unlike a football field, we don't have a referee's whistle to tell us when to stop, when to relax, and when to take a break. Just as Tiger players occasionally get winded during a game, we sometimes find ourselves with our hands on our hips too exhausted emotionally, physically, or psychologically to go on. We need a time out.

That need for a break may even includes our faith life. We are just too tired to go to church this morning or to take up that Bible study tonight. There's just no way we can read a Bible story and say our prayers with the children tonight at bedtime.

The Bible, however, admonishes us not to even think about taking a break from God along our faith journey. Instead, we are told to rejoice always, to never stop praying, and to give thanks whatever is happening in our lives.

God never takes a vacation. He never stops showering us with blessings. He never stops loving us. He's always on the job.

God is not a part-timer; we shouldn't be either.

[Michael Dyer] did a great job to keep himself going. He made a play.
-- Oregon coach Chip Kelly on Dyer's not stopping on the 37-yard run

God never stops; neither should we.

THOSE THINGS

Read John 9:1-11.

"'[T]his happened so that the work of God might be displayed in his life'" (v. 3b).

All set to contend for the NCAA championship, Auburn golfer Buddy Gardner suffered one of those things: a freakish encounter with a light fixture.

As a junior, Gardner, a two-time All-America, led Auburn to the SEC championship in 1976. His stroke average that season was the best in school history; his average in '77 was the second-best ever.

Gardner started playing when he was 4. By the time he was a teenager, he could outdrive every grown man he played against. "I'd swing so hard I'd be facing the other way," Gardner recalled.

He grew up in an Auburn family and said years later that winning the SEC title in '76 was "my greatest thrill as far as a golf accomplishment. We did not have the best talent, but we had more guts on that team than anybody. That's why we won."

The season ended in personal disappointment for Gardner. He was listed among the favorites for the '76 NCAA title, but he never got the chance to play. Shortly before the tournament, he was watching the NBA Finals on TV. When a player hit a long jumper that sent the game into overtime, he jumped off the couch in excitement and hit the ceiling's light fixture. "A piece of glass was coming toward my face and I grabbed it," he recalled. His quick reflexes saved his face, but the glass almost cut his middle finger off. "It was just hanging there," he said. "I had 32 stitches."

Gardner went to the championships in Albuquerque, but broke the stitches on his first swing. He didn't play and eventually had surgery on the finger.

He came back to finish fifth in the NCAA championships of 1977 but lost his chance in 1976 because of one of those things.

You've probably had a few of "those things" in your own life: bad breaks that occur without regard to justice, morality, or fair play. You wonder if everything in life is random with events determined by a chance roll of some cosmic dice. Is there really somebody scripting all this with logic and purpose?

Yes, there is; God is the author of everything.

We know how it all began; we even know how it all will end. It's in God's book. The part we play in God's kingdom, though, is in the middle, and that part is still being revealed. The simple truth is that God's ways are different from ours. After all he's God and we are not. That's why we don't know what's coming our way, and why "those things" catch us by surprise and dismay us when they do occur.

What God asks of us is that we trust him. As the one – and the only one – in charge, he knows everything will be all right for those who follow Jesus.

To this day, I can tell you if it's going to rain.
-- Buddy Gardner on the injury to his middle finger

Life confounds us because, while we know
the end and the beginning of God's great story, we
are part of the middle, which God is still writing.

DAY 61

RECIPE FOR DISASTER

Read Luke 21:5-11, 25-28.

"There will be great earthquakes, famines and pestilences in various places, and fearful events and great signs from heaven" (v. 11).

A simple extra-point attempt turned into an unmitigated disaster for Auburn. Until LSU had a disaster of its own.

The two teams met on Sept. 18, 2004, in what turned out to be a showdown for the SEC West title. LSU, the defending national champion, was undefeated and ranked 4th. Auburn was undefeated and ranked 14th.

LSU led 9-3 when Auburn took over at its own 40 with 6:37 to play. "We've got one shot. Let's get it done," quarterback Jason Campbell told his huddle. What followed was the stuff of Auburn legend. The Tigers moved relentlessly downfield until with 1:14 on the clock, Campbell hit receiver Courtney Taylor with a 16-yard TD strike to tie the game. All Auburn had to do to take the lead was kick its 192nd consecutive extra point. The Tigers had not missed a PAT kick since 1999.

Instead, what was routine was a disaster. The snapper rolled the ball back to holder Sam Rives, and John Vaughn's kick "sailed mercilessly, painfully left." "It was brutal," Rives said. "My heart sank." "I had this awful feeling in the pit of my stomach," said defensive end Bret Eddings, watching from the sideline.

But this extra-point try boasted dual disasters. LSU was flagged on the play "due to a new and relatively obscure rule" that wasn't even in effect the season before. An LSU defender had jumped over the line of scrimmage and landed on the Auburn snapper.

Auburn's kicking unit flirted with disaster again on the second try when the snap again rolled back to Rives. This time, though, he was ready and gathered the ball and set it in position. Vaughn boomed it through the uprights for the game-winning point.

Thanks to LSU's own disaster, Auburn had averted a disaster.

We live in a world that seems to be either struck by one disaster after another or is the home of several ongoing and seemingly permanent disasters. Earthquakes virtually obliterate an entire nation; volcanoes erupt and change the climate; children around the world starve to death every day. Floods devastate cities and shatter lives; oil pollutes our oceans and seashores. Can we even count the number of wars that are going on at any one time?

This apparently unending litany of disaster is enough to make us all give up hope. Maybe – but not for the followers of Jesus Christ. The truth is that Jesus' disciples should find reassurance of their ultimate hope in the world's constant disasters because this is exactly what Jesus said would happen.

These disasters indicate that the time of our redemption is drawing near. How near is up to God to decide. Nevertheless, this is a season of hope and great promise for those of the faith.

Sometimes you just have to have lucky things go your way.
-- Tommy Tuberville on avoiding the PAT disaster against LSU

Jesus told us what to do when disaster threatens
to overwhelm us and our world:
'Stand up and lift up your heads.'

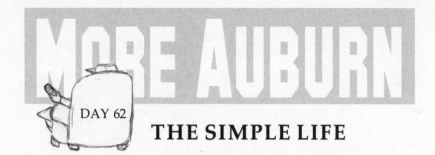

THE SIMPLE LIFE

Read 1 John 1:5-10.

"If we confess our sins, he is faithful and just and will forgive us our sins and purify us from all unrighteousness" (v. 9).

The formula was a simple one -- outstanding defense, excellent kicking, and no mistakes -- but it carried Auburn all the way to an undefeated season and the 1957 national championship.

In the spring of 1957, head coach Shug Jordan realized he had the potential for a solid team though "we had too many sophomores and untried people we were counting on." In the fall, he set out to find the players he could count on, and it was tough.

"You don't get fat playing for Shug," said one observer at a fall practice. Senior guard and team captain Tim Baker recalled that the players didn't get water or ice at practice. Other players and he would "take sweaty towels and squeeze 'em to try and get moisture in our mouth and all we could spit out was cotton."

Several pre-teen boys always showed up for the practices, and the players would slip them a nickel or a dime to sneak in a piece of ice or a cup of water. Ends coach Gene Lorendo caught some of the youngsters in the act one day and made them run a lap.

Jordan was getting his team ready to play basic football with that simple formula. Nowhere was it more efficiently displayed that season than in the opener against Tennessee, the consensus in the preseason to win the conference.

TIGERS

On a rainy day and a sloppy field, Auburn dominated but could score only once. Jerry Wilson blocked a Vol punt, and the Tigers marched 57 yards. Fullback Billy Atkins scored on fourth down from the one and then booted the PAT.

After that, it was "outstanding defense, excellent kicking, and no mistakes." Tennessee moved inside the Auburn 30 three times but couldn't score. Auburn didn't turn the ball over and won 7-0.

Perhaps the simple life in America was doomed by the arrival of the programmable VCR. Since then, we've been on a downward spiral into ever more complicated lives. Windshield wipers have multiple setting, and washing machines look like cockpits.

But we might do well in our own lives to mimic the simple formula that the 1957 Tigers used to win a national title. That is, we should approach our lives with the keen awareness that success requires simplicity, a sticking to the basics: Revere God, love our families, honor our country, do our best.

Theologians may make what God did in Jesus as complicated as quantum mechanics and the infield fly rule, but God kept it simple for us: believe, trust, and obey. Believe in Jesus as the Son of God, trust that through him God makes possible our deliverance from our sins into Heaven, and obey God in the way he wants us to live. It's simple, but it's the true winning formula, the way to win for all eternity.

I think God made it simple. Just accept Him and believe.
-- Bobby Bowden

Life continues to get ever more complicated,
but God made it simple for us
when he showed up as Jesus.

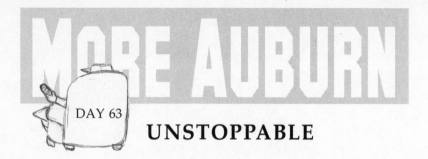

DAY 63

UNSTOPPABLE

Read Acts 5:29-42.

"If it is from God, you will not be able to stop these men; you will only find yourselves fighting against God" (v. 39).

Josh Bynes' durability made him unstoppable on the field. Not even a problem with his shoes could stop him at Media Days.

A senior middle linebacker, Bynes led the national champions of 2010 in tackles. He developed a reputation during the 2009 season as an iron man impervious to pain when he played all year without a backup. In the Outback Bowl against Northwestern that season, even Bynes moved into unchartered territory. Along with outside linebacker Craig Stevens, he was in on all 115 of the Tigers' defensive plays.

In 2010, he just didn't leave the field most Saturdays. He hated water breaks and saw no benefits from rests during a game. "He'll be back there and he might be a little winded, but you'll never know because he's going hard on every play," said defensive end Antoine Carter.

By the time the national title game rolled around, the unstoppable Bynes was being hailed as Auburn's rock. He was called "the player who's been at the center of putting this dream season together" and "the unquestioned leader" of the team.

Bynes' determination to play no matter what even showed up at the 2010 Media Days. Minutes before he was to walk downstairs and face the assembled media, he discovered to his horror that he hadn't packed his dress shoes. No one around him had an extra pair, and he didn't have time to go shopping.

So Bynes did what any unstoppable middle linebacker would do: He went with what he had, striding through the hotel in his coat and tie and flip-flops (much to his teammates' amusement). But he made the interviews.

Like Josh Bynes, the entire Auburn team in 2010 was unstoppable. The Tigers stopped only when they ran out of teams to beat.

Isn't that the way we would like our life to unfold? One success after another in our career, our family, our investments – whatever we tackle. Unstoppable. The reality is, though, that life isn't like that at all. At some point, we all run into setbacks that stop us dead in our tracks. Everyone does – except God.

For almost two thousand years, the enemies of God have tried to stop Jesus and his people. They killed Jesus; they have persecuted and martyred his followers. Today, heretics and infidels – many of them in America -- are more active in their war on Christianity than at any other time in history.

And yet, the Kingdom of God advances, unstoppable despite all opposition. Pursuing God's purposes in our lives puts us on a team bound for glory. Fighting against God gets his enemies nowhere. Except Hell.

He's taken a load on his shoulders and he's just controlling everything and being able to play every snap and not get hurt. It's the best thing.
-- Reserve linebacker Jessel Curry on Josh Bynes in 2010

**God's kingdom and purposes are unstoppable
no matter what his enemies try.**

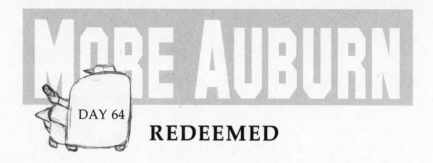
DAY 64

REDEEMED

Read 1 Peter 1:17-25.

"It was not with perishable things such as silver or gold that you were redeemed from the empty way of life handed down to you from your forefathers, but with the precious blood of Christ" (vv. 18-19).

On a chilly January night in Brenham, Texas, of all places, Cam Newton took his first steps toward redemption.

Some eight hundred and fifty miles from home in a town with a population of a few more than 16,000 people at a junior college with about 15,000 students -- that's where Newton found himself in 2009. He was a long way from the bright lights that had shone on him since he first donned his pads to play football. Nearly every school in the SEC had offered him a scholarship; he decided on Florida, "hoping to become the next Tim Tebow."

It didn't turn out that way. In Gainesville, Newton's life unraveled to the point that in 2008 he was charged with stealing a computer. He insisted he had bought it from a man out of the trunk of his car. "It was really too good to be true," he admitted. "It was just a dumb move." The charges were subsequently dropped, but Newton was suspended from the team.

Still, he wanted to stay at Florida and start in 2009. And then Tebow surprised everyone by announcing he would return for his senior season. Newton immediately decided to transfer.

That's how he wound up in Texas, his reputation sullied, his football career hanging by the proverbial thread. Exhausted, scared, and not wanting to talk to anybody, he spent that first night on a couch at the home of his head coach. He didn't know it, but he had arrived in "the unlikely place that would save him."

Newton led Blinn College to the junior college national championship in 2009. A season later, he was at Auburn, his life and his football career redeemed and resurrected. "I'm an example of why people deserve second chances," he said.

In our capitalistic society, we know all about redemption. Just think "rebate" or store or product coupons. To receive the rebates or the discount, though, we must redeem them, cash them in.

"Redemption" is a business term; it reconciles a debt, restoring one party to favor by making amends. In the Bible, a slave could obtain his freedom only upon the paying of money by a redeemer. In other words, redemption involves the cancelling of a debt the individual cannot pay on his own.

While literal, physical slavery is incomprehensible to us today, we nevertheless live much like slaves in our relationship to sin. On our own, we cannot escape from its consequence, which is death. We need a redeemer, someone to pay the debt that gives us the forgiveness from sin we cannot give ourselves.

We have such a redeemer. He is Jesus Christ, who paid our debt not with money, but with his own blood.

I've grown so much as a person in the last two years, and it all goes back to my time in Brenham.
-- Cam Newton in 2010

**To accept Jesus Christ as your savior is to believe
that his death was a selfless act of redemption.**

HEAVENBOUND

Read Revelation 21:1-7.

"Then I saw a new heaven and a new earth, for the first heaven and the first earth had passed away" (v. 1).

Alonzo Horton discovered that a little slice of Heaven exists wherever love abounds -- even during the Tiger Walk.

In 2005, Horton was a redshirted freshman defensive end when Hurricane Katrina hit New Orleans, his hometown. Friday night before Saturday's game, he received a panicked call from a cousin who screamed that water was rushing into the shelter where she and Horton's two younger brothers had sought refuge. They were gone -- swept away.

Saturday was to mark Horton's first-ever Tiger Walk, ordinarily one of the most exhilarating experiences of a freshman's life. As a redshirt, Horton met the bus at the stadium. Head coach Tommy Tuberville was the first to hug him, and players gathered around and cried with him.

But then the band struck up "War Eagle," and the Tiger Walk began. His heart heavy with sorrow, Horton joined his teammates as they followed the cheerleaders through the cheering crowd.

That's when something unexpected happen. From the crowd, someone yelled, "We love you, Alonzo!" Another fan called him over and hugged him. As Horton walked, others called his name and offered him shouts of encouragement, support, and love. He had never played a moment of Auburn football, but they knew who he was and how he was hurting, and they loved him.

Horton later told ESPN, "Every step I took I started to feel better and better. Heaven was at that Tiger Walk."

But there was more to the story. The following Sunday, Horton managed to reach a cousin to pass on the news about his two little brothers. As he talked, the cousin suddenly shouted, "No! They got out! Hold on!" Then to Horton's shock and joy, the cousin handed over the phone and he heard the voices of his brothers.

All too often Christians make the mistake of regarding Heaven as an abstract concept simply because they can't really imagine what's it like. Kind of like trying to figure out what God looks like or what Jesus' voice sounds like. But Heaven is a real place, as substantive as the Tiger Walk, that recliner you watch the Auburn games from, or that lawn mower you use to cut the grass.

The Bible contains only rather limited information about the believer's ultimate destination perhaps because it's much more interested in teaching us how to get there than in describing the lay of the land for us. God's Word is clear, though, that Heaven is a better place than the one we occupy now.

So why can't we have Heaven on Earth? Here, man's will clashes with God's; the result more often than not is chaos, confusion, and tears. In Heaven, though, God's will is achieved absolutely. The result is Paradise.

Heaven is real. You better believe it.

I felt like I was walking to the light.
-- Alonzo Horton on his first Tiger Walk

Heaven is a real place where – unlike here on Earth – God's will is done.

DAY 66

PROVE IT

Read Matthew 3.

"But John tried to deter him, saying, 'I need to be baptized by you, and do you come to me?'" (v. 14)

Kurt Crain showed up in the Loveliest Village in 1985 with a big chip on his shoulder. That's because Auburn didn't believe he was worth recruiting.

A linebacker, Crain played at a time when head coach Pat Dye decided to take the program back to the basics after Bo Jackson left. Before the '86 season, that meant four-a-days for two weeks. "It was so bad," Crain recalled, "after the 8:00 practice, you slept with your tape on so you wouldn't have to get up 30 minutes early to go get your ankles taped.

"It was brutal," Crain said. "We had 30 days in the spring and no limit on how many days you went in pads." He remembered that his forehead would swell up from all the practice and all the hits on his helmet. "All the fluid would drain down into my eyes -- people said I looked like Frankenstein," he said.

It was a time, too, when would-be players quit by the bunches. But not Crain. He had a point to prove.

He wanted to play for Auburn out of high school, but the Tigers didn't recruit him; they said he wasn't big enough. He went to Memphis and decided to transfer after his sophomore season when the coach was killed in a plane crash.

The decision to transfer to Auburn was a hard one. "I proved myself at Memphis in football and baseball," he said. At Auburn, though, he would have to prove himself all over again.

And he did. He led the team in tackles in both 1986 and '87 and was All-SEC both seasons. He was All-America in 1987, the star on defense for the SEC champions. He set the school record for tackles in a game with 26 against Georgia in '86.

Kurt Crain proved he was good enough to play big-time ball.

You, too, have to prove yourself over and over again in your life. To your teachers, to that guy you'd like to date, to your parents, to your bosses, to the loan officer. It's always the same question: "Am I good enough?" Practically everything we do in life is aimed at proving that we are.

And yet, when it comes down to the most crucial situation in our lives, the answer is always a decisive and resounding "No!" Are we good enough to measure up to God? To deserve our salvation? John the Baptist knew he wasn't, and he was not only Jesus' relative but God's hand-chosen prophet. If he wasn't good enough, what chance do we have?

The notion that only "good" people can be church members is a perversion of Jesus' entire ministry. Nobody is good enough – without Jesus. Everybody is good enough – with Jesus. That's not because of anything we have done for God, but because of what he has done for us. We have nothing to prove to God.

I had to go prove myself again and make them regret not recruiting me.
-- Kurt Crain on arriving at Auburn in 1985

The bad news is we can't prove to God
how good we are; the good news is that
because of Jesus we don't have to.

THE CHALLENGE

Read Matthew 4:12-25.

"Come, follow me," Jesus said (v. 19).

His team was undefeated, but an unhappy Gene Chizik challenged some of his players right in front of their teammates.

The offensive line was expected to be one of the strengths of the 2010 Tigers. Four starters returned: guards Mike Berry and Byron Isom, center Ryan Pugh, and tackle Lee Ziemba. Three games into the season, however, the line was "a major disappointment," and after the overtime win over Clemson, Chizik let his hosses know exactly what he thought of their performance. He called them out in a Sunday meeting of the whole team.

While Auburn led the SEC in rushing at the time, QB Cam Newton was the leader with most of his yards coming after he was chased out of the pocket. Against Clemson, the Tigers were two of six on third downs when they needed two yards or less.

Chizik said the line wasn't giving the team the physical play it needed to win championships. Surprisingly, the players agreed. "The truth hurts," Isom said. "We definitely are embarrassed."

How the four senior leaders responded to the challenge is, of course, Auburn legend. Ziemba had an All-American season and won the Jacobs Blocking Trophy as the SEC's best blocker. He set a school record for consecutive starts and was drafted by the Carolina Panthers. Pugh was Third-Team All-America and First-Team All-SEC. Berry was the SEC Lineman of the Week for his game against Georgia. Pugh, Isom and Berry all signed free-agent pro contracts.

As for the team, the undefeated national champs led the SEC in scoring offense, total offense, rushing offense, pass efficiency, first downs, and first down conversions.

Consider the coach's challenge answered.

Like the Auburn Tigers every time they take the field or the court, we are challenged daily. Life is a testing ground, and God intentionally set it up that way. If we are to grow in character, confidence, and perseverance, and if we are to make a difference in the world, we must meet challenges head-on. Few things in life are as boring and as destructive to our sense of self-worth as a job that doesn't offer any challenges.

Our faith life is the same way. The moment we answered Jesus' call to "Come, follow me," we took on the most difficult challenge we will ever face. We are called to be holy by walking in Jesus' footsteps in a world that seeks to render our Lord irrelevant and his influence negligible. The challenge Jesus places before us is to put our faith and our trust in him and not in ourselves or the transitory values of the secular world.

Daily walking in Jesus' footsteps is a challenge, but the path takes us all the way right up to the gates of Heaven – and then right on through.

You definitely won't hear that again from anybody about our offensive line. I'll guarantee that.
*   -- Byron Isom, responding to his coach's challenge*

To accept Jesus as Lord is to joyfully take on the challenge of living a holy life in an unholy world.

DAY 68

TRAGEDY

Read Job 1, 2:1-10.

"In all this, Job did not sin by charging God with wrongdoing" (v. 1:22).

Tragedy forged a championship season for the Tigers of 1983.

On August 20, less than a month before the season opened, the Tigers took part in a team conditioning drill that consisted of four timed 440-yard dashes. Junior fullback Greg Pratt, slated to be the team's starter, had struggled with the drill the year before. He had stayed in Auburn through the summer and worked out to be in the best shape possible. As a result, he made two practice runs without any problem. He passed the physical given to all the players that morning.

The afternoon of the test was hot and humid, and by the third 440, Pratt was struggling. Junior quarterback Randy Campbell recalled that some of the "guys who had finished ran along beside him to encourage him on the last one." Harold Hallman, who would be an All-SEC nose guard in 1985, was one. On the last lap, Hallman held Pratt's hand all the way and helped him finish.

Pratt made his time but he collapsed after finishing the final 440. Campbell recalled that the players didn't think much of it. "I'd collapsed a couple of years earlier," he said. "Usually, four or five guys fell out." That attitude changed, though, when word got around that an ambulance had taken Pratt to the hospital.

Dozens of the players went to the hospital, waiting with the coaches in the hallways. That night, head coach Pat Dye brought them the awful news: Greg Pratt had died. Dye led his team in prayer and told them Pratt had given his life to achieve the high goals they all had.

All season long, the Tigers wore Pratt's number 36 on the back of their helmets as they marched relentlessly to the SEC championship and, according to the *New York Times*, the national title.

While we may receive them in varying degrees, suffering and tragedy are par for life's course. What we do with tragedy when it strikes us – as the story of the 1983 Tigers illustrates – determines to a great extent how we live the rest of our lives.

We can – in accordance with the bitter suggestion Job's wife offered -- "Curse God and die," or we can trust God and live. That is, we can plunge into endless despair or we can lean upon the power of a transcendent faith in an almighty God who offers us hope in our darkest hours.

We don't have to understand tragedy; we certainly don't have to like it or believe there's anything fair about it. What we must do in such times, however, is trust in God's all-powerful love for us and his promise that all things will work for good for those who love him.

In choosing a life of ongoing trust in God in the face of our suffering, we prevent the greatest tragedy of all: that of a soul being cast into Hell.

That tragedy was there all year.

-- Pat Dye on the death of Greg Pratt

**Tragedy can drive us into despair and death or
into the life-sustaining arms of almighty God.**

DAY 69

JUST PERFECT

Read Matthew 5:43-48.

"Be perfect, therefore, as your heavenly Father is perfect"
(v. 48).

One perfectly executed play pretty much finished Georgia off.

The SEC West championship was on the line when the Tigers welcomed the Bulldogs to Jordan-Hare Stadium on Nov. 13, 2010. With a win, Auburn would clinch a berth in the league title game for the first time since 2004.

So how did Auburn do early on? "In the first quarter, we acted like we have never played football before," said linebacker Josh Bynes. The result was three Georgia touchdown passes and a 21-7 lead after the first quarter. "We had to settle down," Bynes said.

They did. The defense upped the pressure on the Dog quarterback and shut down the offense. The Auburn offense meanwhile went to work pounding at the overmatched Georgia defense. Especially in the last half did Auburn "build long, sustained drives that pushed the visiting defense to the brink of exhaustion."

The result was a 21-21 tie at halftime. The play that "changed the game's dynamic" was decided on in the locker room. In reviewing film of the Bulldogs, the Auburn coaches had noticed that the front-line blockers on kickoff returns tended to drop into their blocking formation too early. That meant they were ripe for an onside kick. The coaches decided to go for it.

TIGERS

Wes Byrum was perfect, Georgia was clueless, the ball bounced the required ten yards, and the Tigers recovered it. "That was huge because you kind of steal a drive from them," said wide receiver Emory Blake.

The Tigers took it in to score. The Bulldogs had in effect forfeited a possession because of that perfect play, and they never really recovered. Auburn won going away 49-31.

Nobody's perfect; we all make mistakes every day. We botch our personal relationships; at work we seek competence, not perfection. To insist upon personal or professional perfection in our lives is to establish an impossibly high standard that will eventually destroy us physically, emotionally, and mentally.

Yet that is exactly the standard God sets for us. Our love is to be perfect, never ceasing, never failing, never qualified – just the way God loves us. And Jesus didn't limit his command to only preachers and goody-two-shoes types. All of his disciples are to be perfect as they navigate their way through the world's ambiguous definition and understanding of love.

But that's impossible! Well, not necessarily, if to love perfectly is to serve God wholeheartedly and to follow Jesus with single-minded devotion. Anyhow, in his perfect love for us, God makes allowance for our imperfect love and the consequences of it in the perfection of Jesus.

[The onside kick] swung the momentum in the second half.
-- Gene Chizik on the perfectly executed play

In his perfect love for us, God provides a way
for us to escape the consequences
of our imperfect love for him: Jesus.

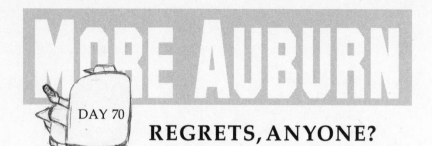

DAY 70

REGRETS, ANYONE?

Read 2 Corinthians 7:8-13.

"Godly sorrow brings repentance that leads to salvation and leaves no regret" (v. 10).

John Powell set school records. He was All-America. He met his wife. All that happened while he was at Auburn, but he still had regrets about his time in the Loveliest Village.

From 1991-94, Powell pitched for the Tigers and terrorized collegiate hitters with a splitter his coach, Hal Baird, described as "devastating. Guys just couldn't hit it."

Powell was a starter from the time he hit the Auburn campus, but as a freshman in 1990 he broke a leg and was redshirted. It turned out to be one of the best things ever to happen to him, for during that time off, Baird and he experimented with the splitter he had tinkered with in high school. When Powell returned for the 1991 season, the pitch was the weapon that made his career.

And it was one of the most outstanding careers in Auburn and collegiate history. Powell set the NCAA record for career strikeouts with 602. He set Auburn records with 43 career wins, with 191 strikeouts in 1993, and with 477 career innings pitched.

In 1993, he was first-team All-America. He was twice first-team All-SEC (1991 and '93) and twice second-team. In 1994, he was the NCAA Regional Tournament MVP.

Along the way, he met a fellow Auburn student who became his wife. "I wouldn't trade it for the world," he once said of his time at Auburn. Even so, he had some regrets.

When he left Auburn, he was convinced a major-league career was his for the taking. It didn't work out that way, though. Elbow problems had plagued him his senior season at Auburn, and they flared up again in Triple-A ball. He left the game for good.

Looking back, Powell regretted he had not taken better care of his body. "You have people telling you what you should do," he said, "but you are setting records and [are] on top of the world. You don't listen like you should."

In their classic hit "The Class of '57," the Statler Brothers served up some pure country truth when they sang, "Things get complicated when you get past 18." That complication includes regrets; you have them; so does everyone else: situations and relationships that upon reflection we wish we had handled differently.

Feeling troubled or remorseful over something you've done or left undone is not necessarily a bad thing. That's because God uses regrets to spur us on to repentance, which is the decision to change our ways. Repentance in turn is essential to salvation through Jesus Christ. You regret your unChristlike actions, repent by promising God to mend your ways, and then seek and receive forgiveness for them.

The cold, hard truth is that you will have more regrets in your life. You can know absolutely, however, that you will never ever regret making Jesus the reason for that life.

Looking back, I probably didn't treat my body as well as I should have.
-- John Powell

Regrets are part of living,
but you'll never regret living for Jesus.

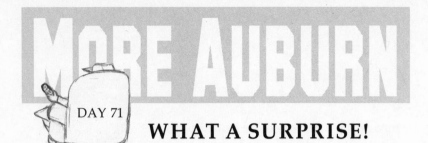

WHAT A SURPRISE!

Read 1 Thessalonians 5:1-11.

*"But you, brothers, are not in darkness so that this day
should surprise you like a thief" (v. 4).*

Assistant coach Eddie Gran wanted to pull a surprise on Virginia Tech. Tommy Tuberville was so reluctant that he told Gran to surprise him too.

The SEC champions led the Hokies 9-0 at halftime of the 2005 Sugar Bowl. That's when Gran, the running backs coach, told his boss the Tigers should catch Tech by surprise with a trick play on the second-half kickoff. Gran suggested "The Globe."

The idea surprised Tuberville. The players had been practicing the unusual kickoff return for a month or so with limited success. "I've been watching y'all run it," Tuberville told Gran, "and it looks [bad] to be honest."

The play called for Carnell Williams to catch the ball and disappear into a gaggle of teammates. He would turn his back to the Tech players and hand the ball off. Then everyone would come flying out, relying on surprise and deception to pull off a big play.

The Tigers still had an outside shot at the national title, and Tuberville, despite his reputation as a coach willing to gamble, was reluctant to take this one. "If we fumble and they get the ball and win this game, you may just lose your job," he told Gran.

But the assistant wouldn't back down. He told his boss, "The kids have practiced it, they're excited about it, they're ready for it."

Tuberville finally relented -- somewhat. He told Gran to make the decision, but to surprise him. He didn't want to know about it.

Gran called it. Despite getting a line-drive, the worst possible kick for the play, the Tigers executed the surprise without a hitch. They returned the ball only to the 22-yard line, though.

Nevertheless, the head coach felt the surprise helped the team. "Our players knew we would do anything we had to do to win the game," he said. And Auburn did win, 16-13.

Some surprises in life provide us with experiences that are both joyful and delightful. Generally, though, we expend energy and resources to avoid most surprises and the impact they may have upon our lives.

For instance, we may be surprised by the exact timing of a baby's arrival, but we nevertheless have the bags packed beforehand and the nursery all set for its occupant. Paul used this very image (v. 3) to describe the Day of the Lord, when Jesus will return to claim his own and establish his kingdom. We may be caught by surprise, but we must still be ready.

The consequences of being caught unprepared by a baby's insistence on being born are serious indeed. They pale, however, beside the eternal effects of not being ready when Jesus returns. We prepare ourselves just as Paul told us to (v. 8): We live in faith, hope, and love, ever on the alert for that great, promised day.

We got the ball, scattered like a bunch of quail and Carlos Rogers took the ball and ran the ball out to the 22-yard line.
-- *Tommy Tuberville on 'The Globe'*

**The timing of Jesus' return will be a surprise;
the consequences should not be.**

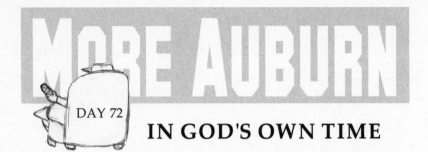

IN GOD'S OWN TIME

Read James 5:7-12.

"Be patient, then, brothers, until the Lord's coming" (v. 7).

When Auburn completed the play that won the 2010 national championship, the clock read 0:00. That's exactly how the patient Tigers planned it.

All season long, Auburn dazzled the opposition with its speed. As writer Tommy Hicks saw it, though, in the BCS national title game against Oregon, the Tigers won "because they had patience."

To take on the Duck defense, offensive coordinator Gus Malzahn drew up an approach for his explosive offense that was dismayingly simple. They would pound the tackles. Then when the Ducks moved their defense up to stop the run, quarterback Cam Newton would drop the ball over the middle or run to the corners.

The scheme bordered on genius when the game unfolded as a defensive struggle. "We just tried to move the football and take some time off the clock," Malzahn said. That threw the Ducks a double whammy: They couldn't stop Auburn and they couldn't get their Day-Glo mitts on the ball to score.

The result of Auburn's patience was 519 yards of total offense. Newton threw for 265 yards and two touchdowns. Offensive MVP Michael Dyer rushed for 143 yards as the Tigers ran the ball fifty times. Terrell Zachery, Darvin Adams, and Emory Blake hauled in a combined fourteen passes for 156 yards.

TIGERS

The result of all that offense was that Auburn won the time of possession by six minutes. The Ducks went one stretch of 37:25 without scoring a point.

Nowhere was that patience more on display than in the game-winning drive. "We just had to go with the flow, one play at a time," Malzahn said. That's exactly what the Tigers did, patiently and seemingly without any sense of urgency moving down the field and using up all the clock for the 22-19 win.

Have you ever left a restaurant because the server didn't take your order quickly enough? Complained at your doctor's office about how long you had to wait? Wondered how much longer a sermon was going to last?

It isn't just the machinations of the world with which we're impatient; we want God to move at our pace, not his. For instance, how often have you prayed and expected – indeed, demanded – an immediate answer from God? And aren't Christians the world over impatient for the glorious day when Jesus will return and set everything right? We're in a hurry but God obviously isn't.

As rare as it seems to be, patience is nevertheless included among the likes of gentleness, humility, kindness, and compassion as attributes of a Christian.

God expects us to be patient. He knows what he's doing, he is in control, and his will shall be done. On his schedule, not ours.

Just getting in field goal range was our goal. At the same time, we didn't want to leave any time on the clock.
-- Gus Malzahn on the patience shown on the game's last drive

God moves in his own time, so often we must wait for him to act, remaining faithful and patient.

DAY 73

STRANGE BUT TRUE

Read Philippians 2:1-11.

"And being found in appearance as a man, he humbled himself and became obedient to death – even death on a cross!" (v. 7)

Auburn might have won the football championship of the collegiate United States at that instant." Strangely enough, the Tigers did it with a play they didn't even have.

After he kicked his starting quarterback off the team before the 1957 season began and the number-two quarterback had left school, head coach Shug Jordan chose Lloyd Nix to compete for the crucial spot. Nix was a 5-11, 175-pound, lefthanded junior who had starred at the position in high school. He had finished his sophomore season at Auburn, though, as the starting right halfback. In September, Jordan simply checked out his stock of available quarterbacks and told Nix, "You're it."

In the season opener against favored Tennessee, the Tigers faced third and six deep in Volunteer territory. "42,000 people shivering under raincoats and umbrellas . . . and 11 Tennessee Volunteers waited to see what [Nix] would do." No one, not even his own teammates, expected what he did.

Nix studied the down marker for a moment, stepped into his huddle, and called, "Thirty-seven, H, Belly." If the other Tigers were surprised, they didn't show it. The play was basically the triple option. What made Nix's call so strange was that it wasn't in Auburn's playbook. It had been discarded -- but Nix called it.

When Nix got the snap from center Jackie Burkett, he faked to fullback Billy Atkins. As a UT linebacker slammed into him, Nix got the ball to right halfback Lamar Rawson, who swept to the four for the first down. Atkins later scored and Auburn won 7-0. The drive to the national championship was under way.

It's strange but it's true: One of the biggest plays in Auburn football history wasn't even in the playbook.

Life is just strange, isn't it? How else to explain tattoos, curling, tofu, and the behavior of teenagers? Isn't it strange that today we have more ways to stay in touch with each other yet are losing the intimacy of personal contact?

And how strange is God's plan to save us? Think a minute about what God did. He could have come roaring down, destroying and blasting everyone whose sinfulness offended him, which, of course, is pretty much all of us. Then he could have brushed off his hands, nodded the divine head, and left a scorched planet in his wake. All in a day's work.

Instead, God came up with a totally novel plan: He would save the world by becoming a human being, letting himself be humiliated, tortured, and killed, thus establishing a kingdom of justice and righteousness that will last forever.

It's a strange way to save the world – but it's true.

Thirty-seven, H, Belly had been dropped from the Auburn arsenal, but Lloyd Nix reached into his mind and found the answer for the moment.
-- Writer Benny Marshall

**It's strange but true: God allowed himself
to be killed on a cross to save the world.**

DAY 74

FAMILY TIES

Read Mark 3:31-35.

*"[Jesus] said, 'Here are my mother and my brothers!
Whoever does God's will is my brother and sister and
mother'" (vv. 34-35).*

For one family, gathering for a photo after the win over South
Carolina in the Georgia Dome was a celebration of not one SEC
championship, but two.

Following Auburn's 56-17 demolition of the Gamecocks on Dec.
4, 2010, the Eddins family joined their thousands of best friends
in the postgame celebration. Naturally, a commemorative photo-
graph was in order, so the family dutifully gathered to capture
the moment. The patriarch of the clan in the snapshot was Liston,
who played defensive end for the Tigers and legendary coach
Shug Jordan from 1973-75.

But that Eddins family photo also includes two of senior's sons
who played on Auburn teams that won football championships.
Bart was a senior reserve offensive lineman on the 2010 national
championship team. His brother, Bret, played defensive end on
Auburn's undefeated 2004 SEC champs.

Bret still harbored the bitter memory of not getting to play
for the national title, so he was especially happy for his brother.
"This opportunity is special and I couldn't be happier," he said.

Bart almost missed the chance himself. He entered the spring
of 2010 hoping to compete for a starting job, having played in

eleven games in 2009, including one start. But then he tore up a knee, and giving up football became an option.

Dad's teachings, though, rescued the season of a lifetime for his son. "Dad always told us, 'Eddins boys never give up,'" Bart said. So he rehabbed the knee and came back.

Bart didn't intentionally ever scan the stands looking for his family during a game, but inevitably he found them and made eye contact at some point. Even before he spotted them, he knew his family was there for him.

Some wit said families are like fudge, mostly sweet with a few nuts. You can probably call the names of your sweetest relatives, whom you cherish, and of the nutty ones too, whom you mostly try to avoid at a family reunion.

Like it or not, you have a family, and that's God's doing. God cherishes the family so much that he chose to live in one as a son, a brother, and a cousin.

One of Jesus' more startling actions was to redefine the family. No longer is it a single household of blood relatives or even a clan or a tribe. Jesus' family is the result not of an accident of birth but rather a conscious choice. All those who do God's will are members of Jesus' family.

What a startling and downright wonderful thought! You have family members out there you don't even know who stand ready to love you just because you're part of God's family.

With us it starts with family and God.

-- Bart Eddins

**For followers of Jesus, family comes not from
a shared ancestry but from a shared faith.**

NUMBER ONE

Read Haggai 1:3-11.

"'You expected much, but see, it turned out to be little. Why?' declares the Lord Almighty. 'Because of my house, which remains a ruin, while each of you is busy with his own house'" (v. 9).

Auburn's first 1000-yard rusher realized what his priorities in life were the day he walked into Hell.

As a senior in 1942, tailback Roy "Monk" Gafford bulldozed his way to 1,004 yards, becoming the first Auburn rusher to break the 1,000-yard mark. He averaged 7.6 yards per carry that season.

Playing in the day of leather helmets and two-way players, Gafford was a proficient kicker, passer, and defender. He was named All-America and the SEC Player of the Year in '42. In 1985, he was inducted into the Alabama Sports Hall of Fame.

Gafford was always uncomfortable with his fame, however. "I'd say I had some sort of complex about the publicity I got," he said years later. "My teammates had as much to do with me making it as I did."

Only months after the 1942 season ended, Gafford was on the front lines of World War II. What he experienced put football in its proper place for him.

In April 1945, Gafford was among the first Allied troops to enter the liberated concentration camp at Dachau. "I was actually the first officer with men taking over Dachau," he recalled. What he saw changed him forever. "You never get over it once you see it," he said. "When you see something like that, it lets you know how important a football game is compared to human life."

Thus, after the war, though Gafford played some professional football, it never was his top priority. He was able to leave the game without regrets and move on with his life.

Like "Monk" Gafford, football may not be the most important thing in your life, but you do have priorities. What is it that you would give up only with your dying breath? Your family? Every dime you have? Your Auburn season tickets?

And what about God? What position does God occupy among your priorities? Which of them would you keep even at the cost of denouncing your faith in Jesus Christ?

God doesn't force us to make such unspeakable choices; nevertheless, followers of Jesus Christ often become confused about their priorities because so much in our lives clamors for attention and time. It all seems so worthwhile.

From God's standpoint, though – the only one that matters – if we work for ourselves and ignore our spiritual lives, we will never have enough. Only our deepest needs matter most to God, and these can be met only through putting God first in our lives. To ignore our relationship with God while meeting our physical needs is to travel down the sure road to death and destruction.

God – and God alone – is No. 1.

If you've ever heard me at a press conference, the first thing I do is give honor to God because he's first in my life.
-- College basketball coach Gary Waters

God should always be number one in our lives.

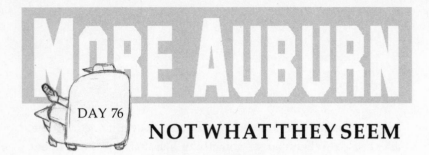
DAY 76

NOT WHAT THEY SEEM

Read Habakkuk 1:2-11.

"Why do you make me look at injustice? Why do you tolerate wrong? Destruction and violence are before me; there is strife, and conflict abounds" (v. 3).

It was just a meager little run up the middle that never made the highlight reels, but the players were convinced it was one of the most spectacular plays of the 2010 national championship season.

In the battle of undefeateds of Oct. 23, Auburn topped LSU 24-17. Onterio McCalebb had a 70-yard TD romp for the game winner, and Cam Newton had a meandering 49-yard scoring run.

Then there was that other play, a simple plunge into the line by tailback Michael Dyer On a second-and-one, Dyer ran between left guard Mike Berry and tight end Phillip Lutzenkirchen. The LSU defense closed quickly, creating a traffic jam. Dyer ducked his head and ploughed on rather than cutting outside.

The freshman was hit after a two-yard gain. He had his first down, so he could simply have gone down and the rest of the offense could have relaxed. What happened instead drove Auburn's fans to their feet and turned Jordan-Hare into a madhouse.

Dyer kept driving his legs, and the pile moved. "Intrigued by the spectacle," center Ryan Pugh and right tackle Brandon Mosley hustled over and began pushing the pile forward. Newton saw what was happening and began pushing as well.

TIGERS

Four Auburn players and five LSU defenders were now in the pile that kept moving forward. Wideouts Kodi Burns and Terrell Zachery broke off their patterns and joined in. Guard Byron Isom left his downfield block to dive in. By the time the pile stopped moving, nine of the eleven Tigers were inside the mass or pushing it from behind.

The play wound up gaining nine yards. "You could just hear the stadium going nuts when we were doing it," Pugh said.

It looked like a simple little play, but it wasn't what it seemed.

Like football, in life sometimes things aren't what they seem. In our violent and convulsive times, we must confront the possibility of a new reality: that we are helpless in the face of anarchy; that injustice, destruction, and violence are pandemic in and symptomatic of our modern age. Anarchy seems to be winning, and the system of standards, values, and institutions we have cherished appears to be crumbling while we watch.

But we should not be deceived or disheartened. God is in fact the arch-enemy of chaos, the creator of order and goodness and the architect of all of history. God is in control. We often misinterpret history as the record of mankind's accomplishments -- which it isn't -- rather than the unfolding of God's plan -- which it is. That plan has a clearly defined end: God will make everything right. In that day things will be what they seem.

As we started to move the pile, this was something like no other.
-- Byron Isom on the play the TV announcer called 'a scrum'

**The forces of good and decency often seem
helpless before evil's power, but don't be fooled:
God is in control and will set things right.**

DAY 77

PLAN AHEAD

Read Psalm 33:1-15.

"The plans of the Lord stand firm forever, the purposes of his heart through all generations" (v. 11).

If the Tigers were to complete their seemingly impossible comeback, they needed a plan. Fortunately, they had one.

When the defending national champions began the 2011 football season against Utah State, they found themselves in a whole bunch of trouble. As the clock ticked away in the fourth quarter, the upstart Aggies held bulldoggedly onto an apparently insurmountable 38-28 lead.

With only 3:38 left in the game, junior quarterback Barrett Trotter put a little life into the team and the crowd by hitting wideouts Emory Blake and Travante Stallworth with consecutive passes that covered 47 yards. On the next play, Trotter found the Aggies in a mistake and made them pay for it. They left tight end Philip Lutzenkirchen all alone, and Trotter gave him some company -- the football. With two minutes left, Auburn trailed 38-35.

Since Utah State had methodically run off long, clock-eating drives the whole game, head coach Gene Chizik had no intentions of giving the Aggies the ball back and hoping his defense could hold. He called for the onside kick.

But he also felt he needed something to surprise the Aggies even if they weren't surprised by the kick. He needed a plan, a kick with a twist. So he called for one. The team's top kickers,

TIGERS

Cody Parkey and Chris Brooks, switched sides just before the kick. That little bit of orchestrated distraction worked.

"I was nervous. I kind of blacked out," Brooks said about the kick. "I was just aiming to get it 10 yards." He did and Blake got the ball. Trotter hit three quick passes to the State 17. Running backs Onterio McCalebb and Michael Dyer took over from there with Dyer getting the touchdown from the 3.

Thanks in large part to a carefully planned and executed kick, the Tigers had a thrilling 42-38 win.

Successful living takes planning. You go to school to improve your chances for a better paying job. You use blueprints to build your home. You plan for retirement. You map out your vacation to have the best time. You even plan your children -- sometimes.

Your best-laid plans, however, sometime get wrecked by events and circumstances beyond your control. The economy goes into the tank; a debilitating illness strikes; a hurricane hits. Life is capricious, and thus no plans -- not even your best ones -- are foolproof.

But you don't have to go it alone. God has plans for your life that guarantee success as God defines it if you will make him your planning partner. God's plan for your life includes joy, love, peace, kindness, gentleness, and faithfulness, all the elements necessary for truly successful living for today and for all eternity. And God's plan will not fail.

If you don't know where you are going, you'll wind up somewhere else.
-- Yogi Berra

Your plans may ensure a successful life;
God's plans will ensure a successful eternity.

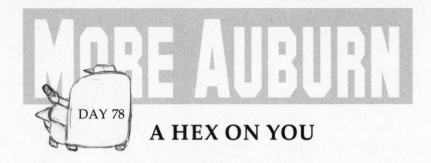

DAY 78

A HEX ON YOU

Read Jonah 1.

"Tell us, who is responsible for making all this trouble for us? What did you do?" (v. 8a)

The Tigers of 2010 were rolling at 6-0. Next up, though, they had to face up to what had become known as The Hawg Hex.

Auburn hosted Arkansas on Oct. 16, and as usual in big games against the Hawgs, the Tigers trailed in the fourth quarter. It's not that Auburn hasn't beaten Arkansas over the years; heading into the 2010 game, Auburn led in the series 10-8-1. It's just that since the school came into the SEC in 1992, Arkansas has shown a distressing tendency to beat the Tigers at the most inopportune times, resulting in "season-wrecking derailings." This had happened so frequently that Van Allen Plexico and John Ringer declared the existence of The Hawg Hex.

The Hex "was in full effect" for the 1995 game. Had Auburn won, they would have been headed for their first SEC championship game. Instead, they lost, missing a game-winning field goal on the final play. The Hawg Hex then "bloomed into full, unquestionable, awful intensity in the back-to-back thrashings of 2001 and 2002" that again cost Auburn trips to Atlanta.

Then there was the 2006 team, one of Auburn's best. The squad won 11 wins including a 17-14 win over Nebraska in the Cotton Bowl. But there it was: a loss to Arkansas that pretty much wiped out hopes of making it to the championship game.

So here the Tigers were again in 2010, the hex rising up in all its gory terror with Arkansas leading 43-37 a minute into the fourth quarter, behind a backup quarterback no less. In five glorious minutes, though, Auburn buried The Hawg Hex forever by scoring four touchdowns on the way to a 65-43 romp in the highest scoring non-overtime game in SEC history.

Hexes and jinxes and the like really belong to the domain of superstitious claptrap. Arkansas has never really had a "hex" on Auburn as the blowout in 2010 shows.

Some people do feel, however, that they exist under a dark and rainy cloud. Nothing goes right; all their dreams collapse around them; they seem to constantly bring about misery on themselves and also on the ones around them.

Why? It is a really a hex?

Nonsense. The Bible provides us an excellent example in Jonah of a person who those around him – namely the sailors on the boat with him -- believed to be a hex. Jonah's life was a mess, but it had nothing to do with a jinx. His life was in disarray because he was disobeying God.

Take a careful look at people you know whose lives are in shambles, including some who profess to believe in God. The key to life lies not just in believing; the responsibility of the believer is to obey God. Life's problems lie not in hexes but in disobedience.

While the Hawg Hex is malevolent and mighty, it may not be strong enough to slow down CamZilla.
-- Plexico and Ringer accurately predicting the end of the Hawg Hex

Hexes don't cause us trouble,
but disobedience to God sure does.

DAY 79

SIZE MATTERS

Read Luke 19:1-10.

"[Zacchaeus] wanted to see who Jesus was, but being a short man he could not, because of the crowd. So he ran ahead and climbed a sycamore-fig tree to see him" (vv. 3-4).

For John Sullen, size mattered. What mattered more than his physical size, though, was the size of his heart and his commitment to Auburn.

The Tigers signed Sullen late in the recruiting process after Gene Chizik was hired in 2008. He had played his senior year of high school at 320 pounds, but when he showed up at Auburn, he hit the groaning scales at 357 pounds. That extra weight meant he couldn't perform at the level expected of an SEC lineman.

Auburn could have just forgotten about him, but offensive line coach Jeff Grimes liked Sullen's footwork and his desire. Grimes gave him some extended playing time in the 54-30 romp over Ball State on Sept. 26, 2009. The coach liked what he saw in Sullen; the kid had talent. There was just too much of him. He went on to play in all thirteen games in '09, but mainly as a blocker on punts.

In Sullen's eyes, that freshman season was pretty much a lost cause because of his weight. "I wish I could have last year back," he said after the season ended.

He committed himself to losing weight. He exercised more than he ever had before and ran quite a bit more than the average lineman typically does. He also overhauled his diet, even learning to stomach the taste of vegetables and grilled items.

When what was to be the national championship season rolled around, Sullen was down to a svelte 305 pounds. His clothes didn't fit, but his football uniform sure did. Plus, he was stronger and quicker than he had ever been. He was a significant contributor, missing only one game with an injury. In 2011, still a smaller man, he moved into the starting lineup.

"Bigger is better" Such is one of the most powerful mantras of our time. We expand our football stadiums. We augment our body parts. Hey, make that a triple cheeseburger and a large order of fries! My company is bigger than your company. Even our church buildings must be bigger to be better. About the only exception to our all-consuming drive for bigness -- as John Sullen discovered -- is our waistlines.

But size obviously didn't matter to Jesus. After all, salvation came to the house of an evil tax collector who was so short he had to climb a tree to catch a glimpse of Jesus. Zacchaeus indeed had a big bank account; he was a big man in town even if his own people scorned him. But none of that – including Zacchaeus' height – mattered; Zacchaeus received salvation because of his repentance, which revealed itself in a changed life.

The same is true for us today. What matters is the size of the heart devoted to our Lord.

It was just something I had to deal with.
-- John Sullen on his extra weight

Size matters to Jesus, but only the size of the heart of the one who would follow Him.

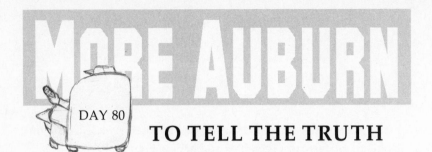

TO TELL THE TRUTH

Read Matthew 5:33-37.

*"Simply let your 'Yes' be 'Yes,' and your 'No,' 'No';
anything beyond this comes from the evil one" (v. 37).*

Blind Bill Turnbeaugh is an Auburn legend, a player so blind he played defense by sound. The truth, however, is not nearly so much fun.

After several down years, Auburn football had disappeared from the national discussion in the early 1950s. The Tigers needed something to get folks talking about them again. Bill Beckwith was just the man for the job.

Beckwith was named Auburn's sports information director in 1951 and managed media relations through Auburn's 1957 national championship season. After the season, he was named ticket manager, a position he manned until his retirement in 1992.

Bill Turnbeaugh was a tackle who lettered at Auburn in 1951 and '52. What made Turnbeaugh extraordinary was not his playing ability. Rather, it was that he wore contact lenses, which weren't widely used in those days, especially by athletes. Those lenses intrigued Beckwith and served as the inspiration for a rather fiendish idea to gain his school some national publicity.

Beckwith created "Blind Bill" Turnbeaugh. "I said that since he couldn't see the other team, he played by ground vibrations," Beckwith said. "He felt them coming." Beckwith called his player's totally imaginary system "hear 'em, feel 'em, and grab 'em." "We got five or six national stories out of Blind Bill," Beckwith said.

He ran into something of a credibility problem, though, when "Blind Bill" intercepted a pass against Clemson. How in the world could a blind man catch a football? Beckwith was up to the challenge, telling reporters Turnbeaugh read ground vibrations to determine that the play was a pass. He saw a blur when the ball came near, and "since it was not wearing an Auburn jersey, he grabbed it."

We live today in an age of barefaced hyperbole, though as the Blind Bill Turnbeaugh legend illustrates, stretching the truth isn't exactly a newfangled concoction.

No, that dress doesn't make you look fat. But, officer, I wasn't speeding. I didn't get the project finished because I've been at the hospital every night with my ailing grandmother.

Sometimes we lie to spare the feelings of others; more often, though, we lie to bail ourselves out of a jam, to make ourselves look better to others, or to gain the upper hand over someone.

But Jesus admonishes us to tell the truth. Frequently in our faith life we fret about what is right and what is wrong, but we can have no such ambivalence when it comes to telling the truth or lying. God and his son are so closely associated with the truth that lying is ultimately attributed to the devil ("the evil one").

Given his character, God cannot lie; given his character, the devil lies as a way of life. Given your character, which is it?

I first sold him to the Associated Press.
-- Bill Beckwith on 'Blind Bill' Turnbeaugh

Jesus declared himself to be the truth,
so whose side are we on when we lie?

DAY 81

A FAST START

Read Acts 2:40-47.

"Everyone was filled with awe. . . . [They] ate together with glad and sincere hearts, praising God and enjoying the favor of all the people" (vv. 43a, 46b, 47a)

Coming off an unranked, five-loss year with an untested, unproven quarterback, the Tigers and their field general needed to get off to a fast start for the 2010 season. They certainly did that.

Cam Newton hit the field against Arkansas State on Sept. 4 as "perhaps the program's most anticipated player in a generation." He was certainly the most hyped, which is rather interesting for a player who hadn't been on the field for an SEC game since the 2008 opener for Florida and had thus far played his college ball at a junior college in Texas. Though he led Blinn College to the national title in 2009, Newton had received notice only as an Honorable Mention All-America.

Nevertheless, Newton was the center of attention and anticipation when the season started at Jordan-Hare. And as one writer put it, "all the hype surrounding Cam Newton was premature." He said the media should have waited for Newton to play a game before writing about how good he was. If they had, "We would have known he was even better than advertised."

Admittedly, the Arkansas State Red Wolves of the Sun Belt Conference didn't exactly approach the level of the likes of LSU, Alabama, Arkansas, and Georgia. But there was no doubting that

TIGERS

Newton more than lived up to the hype.

He threw for three touchdowns and ran for two more in the 52-26 romp. He passed for 186 yards and rushed for 171 more, the latter a single-game record for AU quarterbacks, breaking Phil Gargis' 1974 mark. Newton set everyone abuzz in the second quarter when he ripped off a 71-yard touchdown run on a planned draw.

Overall, the whole team got off to the fast start that it needed, scoring 35 points in the first half.

Fast starts are crucial for more than football games and races. Any time we begin something new, we want to get out of the gate quickly and jump ahead of the pack and stay there as Cam Newton and the Tigers did in 2010.

This is true for our faith life also. For a time after we accepted Christ as our savior, we were on fire with a zeal that wouldn't let us rest, much like the early Christians described in Acts. All too many Christians, however, let that blaze die down until only old ashes remain. We become lukewarm pew sitters.

The Christian life shouldn't be that way. Just because we were tepid yesterday doesn't mean we can't be boiling today. Every day we can turn to God for a spiritual tune-up that will put a new spark in our faith life; with a little tending that spark can soon become a raging fire. Today could be the day our faith life gets off to a fast start – again.

Being his first football game, I couldn't be prouder of what he did.
-- Gene Chizik on Cam Newton vs. Arkansas State

**Every day offers us yet another chance
to get off to a fast start for Jesus.**

NOISEMAKER

Read Psalm 100.

"Shout for joy to the Lord, all the earth!" (v. 1)

So just how did the SEC champions of 2004 prepare for the noise they would encounter when they played before 107,000 rabid Tennessee fans in Knoxville? They ignored it.

After the legendary 10-9 win over LSU, the 8th-ranked Tigers had to face the 10th-ranked Volunteers on the road. They knew they would be up against "the largest and loudest stadium they would face all season." Still, they approached the hostile environment with something resembling nonchalance.

Head coach Tommy Tuberville refused to get caught up in the media hoopla about the noise in Knoxville. "I don't think it serves any purpose," he said, to fixate on factors his team couldn't control. So at practice, instead of playing recorded crowd noise at numbing levels, Tuberville and his coaches spent the week talking about focus and communication. "We've been to several stadiums before that are very noisy," he said. "It just takes a lot more concentration."

The Tigers absolutely refused to change anything about their approach to the game because of the noise. Offensive coordinator Al Borges told quarterback Jason Campbell just to treat the game like any other when it came to changing plays at the line.

Campbell nicely summarized how his team wanted to handle the crowd noise. "Coming into a place like Tennessee," he said, the Tigers wanted "to try and make some plays and get their crowd out of the game" early on.

One play pretty much did that. With the game scoreless and Auburn sitting at the UT goal line, Ronnie Brown went off right tackle and met a Tennessee safety head-on. The Auburn tailback hit the defender so hard the Volunteer's helmet flew off as Brown powered his way in for the game's first touchdown.

Auburn led 31-3 at halftime, and all that deafening noise had been replaced by "a hushed gloom."

Whether you're at an Auburn game live or watching on TV, no doubt you've contributed to the crowd noise generated by thousands of fans or just your buddies. You've probably been known to whoop it up pretty good at some other times in your life, too. The birth of your first child. The concert of your favorite band. That fishing trip when you caught that big ole bass.

But how many times have you ever let loose with a powerful shout to God in celebration of his love for you? Though God certainly deserves it, he doesn't require that you walk around waving pompoms and shouting "Yay, God!" He isn't particularly interested in having you arrested as a public menace.

No, God doesn't seek a big show or a spectacle. A nice little "thank you" is sufficient when it's delivered straight from the heart and comes bearing joy. That kind of noise carries all the way to Heaven; God hears it even if nobody else does.

Loud is loud. Anywhere you go, it's loud.
-- Receiver Anthony Mix on playing in Knoxville

The noise God likes to hear is a heartfelt "thank you," even when it's whispered.

FOR THE FUN OF IT

Read Nehemiah 8:1-12.

"Do not grieve, for the joy of the Lord is your strength"
(v. 10c).

Since he's a "chest-bumping, towel-waving dynamo," Trooper Taylor is easy to spot on the Auburn sideline. He's the one who seems to be having more fun than everybody else.

Taylor joined Gene Chizik's staff in 2009 as the team's assistant head coach and the wide receivers coach. He's such an excellent recruiter that Rivals.com has repeatedly named him to its annual list of the country's top 25 recruiters.

On top of his official duties, Taylor is the "players' big brother on campus, cheerleader and keep-it-loose guy." He's the one who had quarterback Cam Newton and other players over to his home before the 2010 Christmas break and put them to making gingerbread houses. He made Newton do his over.

Taylor is almost certainly the most visible of all the Auburn assistant coaches. He's the one who believes football should be fun and acts like it on the sideline. His trademark is his towel, which he has kept hanging off his belt since the seventh grade purely for celebratory purposes. Now he uses it to excite the crowd. "When I wave that towel, that crowd goes absolutely crazy, and then the players get into it," Taylor said.

Taylor is also the master of the sideline chest bump, though he quickly became wary of clashing flesh with Newton. "He hit me and my hat came off and my head phones went flying," Taylor recalled. "But he didn't knock me down."

Taylor consciously worked in 2010 to make practice just a tad more fun. For instance, he daily flipped a piece of gum to tight end Philip Lutzenkirchen, who caught it in his mouth. "It's something silly, but it's fun to him," Taylor said. The routine also included a hug and high-five shared with deep snapper Josh Harris.

It all contributed to the fun of a national championship.

A very erroneous stereotype of the Christian lifestyle has emerged, that of a dour, sour-faced person always on the prowl to sniff out fun and frivolity and shut it down. "Somewhere, sometime, somebody's having fun – and it's got to stop!" Many understand this to be the mandate that governs the Christian life.

But God's attitude toward fun is clearly illustrated by Nehemiah's instructions to the Israelites after Ezra had read God's commandments to them. They broke out into tears because they had failed God, but Nehemiah told them not to cry but to go eat, drink, and be merry instead. Go have fun, believers! Celebrate God's goodness and forgiveness!

This is still our mandate today because a life spent in an awareness of God's presence is all about celebrating, rejoicing, and enjoying God's countless gifts, especially salvation in Jesus Christ. To live for Jesus is to truly know the fun in living.

Football's a game, and I think a lot of people get confused and take the fun out of the game.

-- Trooper Taylor

**What on God's wonderful Earth
can be more fun that living for Jesus?**

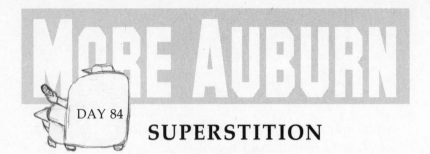

DAY 84

SUPERSTITION

Read Isaiah 2:6-16.

"They are full of superstitions from the East; . . . they bow down to the work of their hands" (vv. 6b, 8b).

Over the course of his career and especially during the 2010 season, the superstitions "piled up to ridiculous proportions" for Auburn's All-American offensive tackle Lee Ziemba (2007-10).

For instance, most players slide their jerseys over their shoulder pads and put them both on at the same time. Ziemba, however, always put his shoulder pads on first and then asked a teammate to help him pull the jersey on, a practice left guard Mike Berry called "strange." "I've helped him a few times," Berry said. "I've also told him no, to do it himself." It wasn't just the pads, though. Ziemba put every stitch of football clothing on in exactly the same way and in exactly the same order every single time.

But there was more. Before the team stretched in the locker room, Ziemba put his fingers in the earholes of his helmet, flipped it twice, placed it on its right side, stacked his left glove on top of it first, and finished off with his right glove. If at any time during the stretching either glove fell off, "Whew, I'm not a happy guy," Ziemba said.

The rituals continued on the field. At the same time every game, he threw half a cup of water to his right. A graduate assistant had to hold his gloves for a certain time, those same gloves he wouldn't wear inside.

Perhaps the most bizarre superstition arose in 2010 arose after Berry decided to mess with Ziemba's mind. He stole the tackle's knee pads out his locker and did it for several weeks until Ziemba caught him. Berry sheepishly returned the pads but Ziemba freaked out. "I'm going to turn my back and you steal them," he said. And Berry did every week, as long as Auburn kept on winning, which, of course, was all season.

Superstitions -- such as wideout Emory Blake's insistence on wearing two wrist bands on his right arm -- can be quite benign. Nothing in the Bible warns us about the dangers inherent in walking under ladders or not putting our clothes on a certain way.

God is quite concerned, however, about superstition of a more serious nature such as using the occult to predict the future. Its danger for us is that we allow something other than God to take precedence in our lives; we in effect worship idols.

While most of us scoff at palm readers and psychics, we nevertheless risk being idol worshippers of a different sort. Just watch the frenzied reaction of fans when a movie star or a star football player shows up. Or consider how we often compromise what we know is right merely to save face or to gain favor in the workplace.

Superstition is the stuff of nonsense. Idol worshipping, however, is as real for us today as it was for the Israelites. It is also just as dangerous.

It's disgusting, really. Really, it's creepy, that's what it is.
-- Lee Ziemba on his superstitions

Superstition in the form of idol worship
is alive and well today, occurring anytime
we venerate anything other than God.

DAY 85

TIME FOR A CHANGE

Read Romans 6:1-14.

"Just as Christ was raised from the dead through the glory of the Father, we too may live a new life" (v. 4).

From tuba player to football player was a big change for David Campbell, and he made it thanks in part to his mother's change of heart.

Campbell was an All-American defensive tackle in 1968. He was also a two-time All-SEC selection. *Sports Illustrated* named the Auburn junior its National Lineman of the Week after his play in the Tigers' 31-6 romp over fifth-ranked Miami. He was the Most Valuable Lineman in Auburn's 34-10 win over Arizona in the Sun Bowl in '68.

But the young David Campbell didn't start out to be a football player. Instead, he had his heart set on playing baseball and marching in the band in high school. "My dream was always baseball," he recalled. "That was what I was best at." But he was a big guy, which fit right in with playing the sousaphone, a type of tuba modified for the marching band.

Campbell was indeed playing that big tuba in the high school band, but his size drew some interest from the football coaches. So one night -- against his mother's expressed wishes -- he slipped off and went out for football. His secret came out shortly there-after, though, when his mom went to a game expecting to watch her son play in the band. At the game, his two older sisters ratted him out when they spotted him on the sidelines in a football uniform rather than in the stands with the band.

Despite being an eighth grader, Campbell was good enough to play that night. When he trotted onto the field, his bandmates "cheered for me because their ex-tuba player got into the game."

And his mom's reaction? She "realized it was kind of a done deal, so she didn't get mad at me." His mother's change of heart, though, made a major change in David Campbell's life a whole lot easier.

Anyone who asserts no change is needed in his or her life just isn't paying attention. Every life has doubt, worry, fear, failure, frustration, unfulfilled dreams, and unsuccessful relationships in some combination. The memory and consequences of our past often haunt and trouble us.

Recognizing the need for change in our lives, though, doesn't mean the changes that will bring about hope, joy, peace, and fulfillment will occur. We need some power greater than ourselves or we wouldn't be where we are.

So where can we turn to? Where lies the hope for a changed life? It lies in an encounter with the Lord of all Hope: Jesus Christ. For a life turned over to Jesus, change is inevitable. With Jesus in charge, the old self with its painful and destructive ways of thinking, feeling, loving, and living is transformed.

A changed life is always only a talk with Jesus away.

Change is an essential element of sports, as it is of life.
-- Erik Brady, USA Today

**In Jesus lie the hope and the power
that change lives.**

DAY 86

HANGING IN THERE

Read Mark 14:32-42.

"'Father,' he said, 'everything is possible for you. Take this cup from me. Yet not what I will, but what you will'" (v. 36).

While it's certainly true to say the Tigers "won" the first South-Carolina game of 2010, it is perhaps more appropriate to say they "survived" it. They refused to quit until they had a win.

Auburn had a lot go wrong in the contest of Sept. 18 at Jordan-Hare. (See Devotion No. 26.) The biggest problem was a 20-7 USC lead late in the second quarter. The Gamecocks were good; they were ranked twelfth in the nation and would win the SEC East. They were not at all interested in letting Auburn up off the turf. It would have been a good time for the Tigers to give up a little bit.

As head coach Gene Chizik put it, though, "We've got a lot of guys on this team that are relentless." So instead of quitting, the Tigers simply turned their intensity up a notch. They kept playing and they kept playing harder.

It showed in the third quarter when "Auburn didn't seem tired. It seemed tough." The Tigers dominated the quarter, running 32 plays to South Carolina's six -- and "running" was the key word. Auburn bulled its way to 334 rushing yards against a defense that strolled in giving up only 60 yards on the ground per game.

A key part of that relentless ground attack was tailback Michael Dyer, who ran 23 times for 100 yards. He knew beforehand that he was in for a rough night when Chizik asked him prior to the game if he could carry the ball twenty times. Dyer responded, "Are you kidding me?" "He got a little stronger as the game went along," Chizik said. The whole team did. Auburn scored two touchdowns in the final period, the last score coming at the end of a nine-play drive that featured eight running plays.

"These guys are clawing, scratching to find a way to win every week," Chizik said. Against South Carolina, all that scratching, clawing, and persistence netted a 35-27 win.

Life is tough; it inevitably beats us up and kicks us around some. But life has four quarters, and so here we are, still standing, still in the game. Like the Tigers, we know that we can never win if we don't finish. We emerge as winners and champions only if we never give up, if we just see it through.

Interestingly, Jesus has been in the same situation. On that awful night in the garden, Jesus understood the nature of the suffering he was about to undergo, and he begged God to take it from him. In the end, though, he yielded to God's will and surrendered his own.

Even in the matter of persistence, Jesus is our example. As he did, we push doggedly and determinedly ahead – following God's will for our lives -- no matter how hard it gets. And we can do it because God is with us.

Never count us out. We're never going to stop playing football.
– All-American tackle Lee Ziemba after the USC game

It's tough to keep going no matter what,
but you have the power of almighty God
to pull you through.

THE GRUDGE

Read Matthew 6:7-15.

"If you forgive men when they sin against you, your heavenly Father will also forgive you. But if you do not forgive men their sins, your Father will not forgive your sins" (vv. 14-15).

Tommy (T.J.) Jackson made a trip to offer his father forgiveness. While he was on it, his father saved his life.

A 300-lb. noseguard, Jackson was first-team All-SEC as a junior for the SEC champions of 2004. He was second-team All-SEC in 2005. He had grown up in a single-parent home, and during the summer of 2004, he revealed to Chette Williams, the team chaplain, how bitter he still was about his father's deserting him. Williams told the junior that the hatred he carried for his father was keeping him from being an effective Christian. "You need to go see your father and forgive him," he said.

So Jackson called his father and arranged a meeting at his grandmother's house. They sat on the front porch of the house and talked, neither one sure what to say. While they struggled to find the right words, an argument broke out on the street. A gun was fired, and Jackson's father instinctively jumped in front of his son. He was struck by the bullet. Jackson held his father in his arms until the ambulance arrived and then rode with him to the hospital. The wound was serious, but Jackson's dad survived.

While Jackson, Sr., recovered in the hospital, the two grew

closer. But when Jackson's father was released, he fell back into his old problems with addiction, and the son's hopes for a close, lasting relationship were disappointed.

That September during a team prayer meeting, Jackson told his story. Through it all, he said, his faith in God grew as he discovered the liberating power of forgiveness. The football players prayed for their teammate and his father and hugged him, offering him support but also using the power of the Holy Spirit to strengthen each other and to unify the team.

It's probably pretty easy for you to recall times when somebody did you wrong. Have you held insistently onto your grudges so that the memory of each injury still drives up your blood pressure? Or have you forgiven that other person for what he or she did to you and shrugged it off as a lesson learned?

Jesus said to forgive others, which is exactly the sort of thing he would say. Extending forgiveness, though, is monumentally easier said than done. But here's the interesting part: You are to forgive for your sake, not for the one who injured you. When you forgive, the damage is over and done with. You can move on with your life, leaving the pain behind. The past – and that person -- no longer has power over you.

Holding a grudge is a way to self-destruction. Forgiving and forgetting is a way of life – a godly life.

It wasn't about me or my dad. It was about God. It was an awakening for me, and it helped me understand why God has us here.
-- T.J. Jackson on forgiving his father

**Forgiving others frees you from your past,
turning you loose to get on with your life.**

DAY 88

DANCING MACHINE

Read 2 Samuel 6:12-22.

"David danced before the Lord with all his might, while he and the entire house of Israel brought up the ark of the Lord with shouts and the sound of trumpets" (vv. 14-15).

Tight end Philip Lutzenkirchen became an instant Auburn legend with his game-winning reception in the 2010 Iron Bowl. He also became a YouTube sensation for his unfortunate dance that followed the catch.

With 11:55 left in the Alabama game of Nov. 26, sophomore Lutzenkirchen made his only catch of the night, one that "will be replayed for eternity in Iron Bowl circles." From the Alabama 7, Cam Newton took the snap and faked a handoff. He then moved to his right. Lutzenkirchen drifted across the field to the left side and found himself wide open. Newton spotted him and lobbed a pass across the field.

Praying he wouldn't drop it, Lutzenkirchen hauled in the pass for the touchdown that, coupled with Wes Byrum's extra point, gave Auburn a 28-27 lead. The score stood up.

The play was planned; what happened next wasn't. Lutzenkirchen "waltzed toward the back of the end zone, kicking his legs out to the side in a little jig." He later confessed, "I was so excited I really didn't know what I was doing."

His stunned teammates never did find words to describe what was ultimately determined to be a dance of some sort. Tackle Lee

Ziemba called it "the leprechaun dance." Right guard Byron Isom said, "It looked like a Riverdance to me." Offensive coordinator Gus Malzahn's reaction was, "What was that?"

Whatever it was, Lutzenkirchen's "dance" was a big hit on You-Tube under "Teach me how to Lutzie." The Lutzie stands little chance of showing up again, though, because of the grief Lutzen-kirchen caught from his teammates and friends.

One of the more enduring stereotypes of the Christian is of a sour-faced person on the prowl to sniff out fun and frivolity like Philip Lutzenkirchen's dance and shut it down. "Somewhere, sometime, somebody's having fun – and it's got to stop!" Many understand this to be the mandate that governs the Christian life.

But nothing could be further from reality. Ages ago King David, he who would eventually number Jesus Christ among his house and lineage, set the standard for those who love and worship the Lord when he danced in the presence of God with unrestrained joy. Many centuries and one savior later, David's example today reminds us that a life spent in an awareness of God's presence is all about celebrating, rejoicing, and enjoying God's countless gifts, including salvation in Jesus Christ.

Yes, dancing can be vulgar and coarse, but as with David, God looks into our hearts to see what is there. Our very life should be one long song and dance for Jesus.

I hope it doesn't. I really hope it doesn't.
*   -- Philip Lutzenkirchen, asked if his Iron-Bowl dance will catch on*

While dancing and music can be vulgar and obscene, they can also be inspiring expressions of abiding love for God.

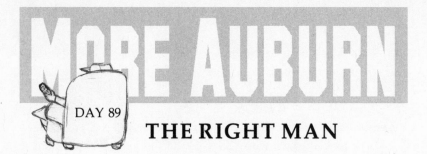

THE RIGHT MAN

Read Exodus 3:1-12.

"So now, go. I am sending you to Pharaoh to bring my people the Israelites out of Egypt" (v. 10).

I t's just my job to catch it when they throw it to me." So declared Auburn wide receiver Darvin Adams. What he did in the 2010 SEC championship game demonstrated clearly that he was the right man for the job.

In his two seasons in residence at the Loveliest Village (2009 and 2010), the 6-foot-3 Adams actually had a pretty good career. With 60 receptions as a sophomore and 53 more in the national championship season, he became the only player in AU history to have two seasons of more than 900 receiving yards.

Despite that record-setting success with his hands, Adams was well known among his teammates for his skills as a blocker. Against South Carolina, though, on Dec. 4, 2010, Adams did what a receiver's job is first and foremost -- catch the ball -- better than anyone in the game's history. Which is odd because Adams didn't catch a pass the last half. Instead, he labored as a blocker as the Tigers romped to the league title with a 56-17 crushing.

In the first half, though, Adams forever cemented his reputation as a receiver. He caught seven passes for 217 yards and two touchdowns. Those 217 yards constituted a new SEC championship game record, easily breaking the old mark of 171 yards.

Adams' 62-yard catch and run set up Auburn's first touchdown.

He followed that up with a 52-yard touchdown nab late in the first quarter that propelled the Tigers into a 21-7 lead.

But Adams wasn't through. He pulled off the most spectacular play of the season on the half's last play by snagging a deflected Hail Mary from Cam Newton in the end zone for a 51-yard touchdown. (See Devotion No. 42.) South Carolina never recovered.

For the national champions, Darvin Adams was the right man for the job.

What do you want to be when you grow up? Somehow you are supposed to know the answer to that question when you're a teenager, the time in life when both common sense and logic are at their lowest ebb. Long after those halcyon teen years are left behind, you may make frequent career changes. You chase the job that gives you not just financial rewards but also some personal satisfaction and sense of accomplishment.

God, too, wants you in the right job, one that he has designed specifically for you. Though Moses protested that he wasn't the right man, he was indeed God's anointed one, the right man to do exactly what God needed done.

There's a little Moses in all of us. Like him, we shrink before the tasks God calls us to. Like him also, we have God-given abilities, talents, and passions. The right man or women for any job is the one who works and achieves not for self but for the glory of God.

I was just trying to make my catches.
-- Darvin Adams on his job on the football field

Working for God's glory and not your own
makes you the right person for the job,
no matter what it may be.

DAY 90

FAMILY TRADITION

Read Mark 7:1-13.

"You have let go of the commands of God and are holding on to the traditions of men" (v. 8).

One of Auburn's most endearing traditions didn't exactly die in 2013 but it sure changed.

On Saturday, April 20, thousands of fans followed up the A-Day game by congregating at Toomer's Corner to drape the oak trees in toilet paper for one last time. Poisoned by an Alabama fan, the two doomed, frail trees were cut down several days after the celebratory tribute that marked the end of an Auburn tradition.

Exactly when the tradition began of celebrating Auburn victories with toilet paper at Toomer's Corner has been lost to time, but it's generally accepted that it carries back to the 1960s. Rolling Toomer's Corner didn't begin with the oak trees but rather with the utility wires across the intersection. As retired Auburn athletic director David Housel recalled it, only after the wires were buried did Auburn fans start rolling the trees sometime in the late 1970s or early 1980s.

Cutting down the beloved oaks was actually a move necessary to preserving the tradition, a first step in renovating Toomer's Corner. Interestingly, before construction of the new design began, a temporary wiring system was installed. "This is kind of going back" to the original tradition, observed Kevin Cowper, Auburn's assistant city manager.

"Traditions change. All things human change," Housel declared. "Auburn is more than two oak trees." So did this unique Auburn tradition change, but as alumni association president Bill Stone said, "We'll be here and we're gonna roll and roll this corner just as we always have and just as we always will."

You encounter traditions practically everywhere in your life. Your workplace may have casual Friday. Your family may have a particular way of decorating the Christmas tree, or it may gather to celebrate Easter at a certain family member's home.

Your church probably has traditions also. A particular type of music, for instance. Or how often you celebrate Communion. Or the order of worship.

Jesus knew all about religious tradition; after all, he grew up in the Church. He understood, though, the danger that lay in allowing tradition to become a religion in and of itself, and in his encounter with the Pharisees, Jesus rebuked them for just that.

Obviously Jesus changed everything that the world had ever known about faith. That included the traditions that had gradually arisen to define the way the Jews of his day worshipped. Jesus declared that those who truly worship God do not do so by simply observing various traditions, but instead by establishing a meaningful, deep-seated personal relationship with him.

Tradition in our faith life is useful only when it helps to draw us closer to God.

Something doesn't have to be old to be a tradition.
-- Auburn Alumni Association President Bill Stone

**Religious tradition has value only when it
serves to strengthen our relationship with God.**

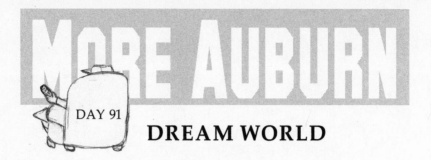

DAY 91

DREAM WORLD

Read Joshua 3.

"All Israel passed by until the whole nation had completed the crossing on dry ground" (v. 17b).

No scholarship offers, twenty years old, stuck at home, almost two years away from the field. Cameron Artis-Payne's dream of playing big-time college football was dead. Well, maybe not.

Artis-Payne had a big season as a senior running back in Pennsylvania in 2007. What he didn't have was a track record beyond that. Or decent grades. He also didn't have any scholarship offers after his senior year ended. So to pull his grades up and to gain some more experience, he enrolled in a prep school in New York in 2008. Again, no offers came his way.

About then, Artis-Payne's dreams about playing any more football were pretty fanciful. He turned 20 living at home, working out, and hoping and dreaming. That was it.

Until he received a phone call. In a casual conversation, a coach from a California junior college mentioned to one of Artis-Payne's old high-school coaches that they needed a running back. The coach told them about his former player and then called Artis-Payne and asked him if he wanted to head West. The coach didn't have to ask twice.

Artis-Payne finally had the chance to make his dream come true, and he didn't waste it. In 2011, he rushed for 1,364 yards and then topped that with a school-record 2,048 yards in 2012.

TIGERS

The recruiters came calling, and he was widely mentioned as the No.-1 junior college running back in the country.

Picking a school was easy. He wanted to play in the SEC against the best, and when Auburn offered a scholarship, he took it. Thus, Cameron Artis-Payne completed his long journey to big-time football in the 2013 A-Day game, rolling up 164 all-purpose yards and scoring a touchdown. His apparently shattered dream, once dead and buried, had come true.

No matter how tightly or doggedly we cling to our dreams, devotion to them won't make them a reality. Moreover, the cold truth is that all too often dreams don't come true even when we put forth a mighty effort. The realization of dreams generally results from a head-on collision of persistence and timing.

But what if our dreams don't come true because they're not the same dreams God has for us? That is, they're not good enough and, in many cases, they're not big enough.

God calls us to great achievements because God's dreams for us are greater than our dreams for ourselves. Could the Israelites, wallowing in the misery of slavery, even dream of a land of their own? Could they imagine actually going to such a place?

The fulfillment of such great dreams occurs only when our dreams and God's will for our lives are the same. Our dreams should be worthy of our best – and worthy of God's involvement in making them come true.

I was still in shape, and I was ready to play right away.
-- Cameron Artis-Payne on how he kept his dream alive

If our dreams are to come true, they must be worthy of God's involvement in them.

DAY 92

THE END

Read Revelation 22:1-17.

*"I am the Alpha and the Omega, the First and the Last,
the Beginning and the End" (v. 13).*

In the end, Bobby Hoppe found his peace about the night that tormented him for decades, the night he killed a man.

As a senior, Hoppe was the right halfback and a defensive back for the 1957 national champions. He was an All-SEC star.

That dream season was preceded, however, by a nightmare. One night, a car tried to run Hoppe off the road, and he recognized a reputed bootlegger who was his sister's ex-lover. The car pulled alongside him, and the driver pointed a pistol at Hoppe. He grabbed his shotgun, fired it without aiming, and sped off. The next morning he learned that the driver was dead.

Hoppe kept his secret for more than thirty years. When rumors spread in 1987 that the case was being reopened, he confessed to his wife, Sherry Lee, that he had indeed killed a man. He was indicted for first-degree murder in March 1988; the trial made headlines across the country. His attorney argued self-defense; the jury deadlocked 10-2 for acquittal, and Hoppe was never retried. He died in 2008; he was 73.

According to his wife, the shooting tormented Hoppe most of his life. "He suffered so much keeping that terrible secret inside," she said. "He told me, 'I'd look in the mirror as I shaved and I'd see this man with his face blown off.'"

The trial didn't bring closure or peace overnight for Hoppe. "He did feel some relief," his wife said about the ordeal of the trial. "He had looked the world in the eye and told the truth."

The peace Hoppe sought for so long finally came during a pilgrimage to Israel in 2000. "He walked where Jesus walked and he found peace," his wife said, "but he prayed for [the soul of the man he killed] 'till the day he died."

Bobby Hoppe's life provides an illustration of one of the basic truths of our existence: Everything ends, even personal torment. The stars have a life cycle, though admittedly it's rather lengthy. Erosion eventually will wear a boulder to a pebble. Life itself is temporary; all living things have a beginning and an end.

Within the framework and the decades of our individual lifetimes, we experience endings. Loved ones, friends, and pets die; relationships fracture; jobs dry up; our health, clothes, lawn mowers, TV sets – they all wear out. In accordance with God's plan for redemption, even this world as we know it will end.

But one of the greatest ironies of God's gift of life is that not even death is immune from the great truth of creation that all things must end. That's because through Jesus' life, death, and resurrection, God himself acted to end any power death once had over life. In other words, because of Jesus, the end of life has ended. Eternity is ours for the claiming.

He finally accepted God's forgiveness, and he was finally able to forgive himself.
-- Sherry Lee Hoppe on her husband's finding peace in the end

**Everything ends; thanks to Jesus Christ,
so does death.**

THE END   187

MORE AUBURN

NOTES
(by Devotion Day Number)

1 only a few dozen more than the infamous 3-2 win over MSU two seasons before.: Evan Woodbery, "Defense Dominates," *All in to Win* (Birmingham: *The Birmingham News*, 2011), p. 70.

1 The Auburn offense "could do nothing but . . . defensive counterparts went to work.": Andy Staples, "A Defense to Lean On," *Sports Illustrated Presents Auburn Tigers: Pride of the Plains* (New York City: Time, Inc., 2011), p. 15.

1 Nick Fairley and linebacker Josh . . . and sang "Lean on Me": Staples, "A Defense to Lean On."

1 That's what we've got . . . got to lean on each other.: Staples, "A Defense to Lean On."

2 "the best offense around,": Charles Goldberg, "Auburn Defense Does the Job," *All in to Win* (Birmingham: *The Birmingham News*, 2011), p. 16.

2 they had given up "more estate than Donald Trump owns.": Bill Bryant, "Not a Flinch," *All in to Win* (Birmingham: *The Birmingham News*, 2011), p. 31.

2 "The thing about this group is when they're challenged they've responded,": Goldberg, "Auburn Defense Does the Job," p. 16.

2 For weeks on end, . . . to recognize things,": Goldberg, "Auburn Defense Does the Job," p. 16.

2 "Oregon's futility near the red . . . frustrating memories" of the game.: Evan Woodbery, "Grading the Tigers," *All in to Win* (Birmingham: *The Birmingham News*, 2011), p. 19.

2 "I feel like we earned a lot of respect tonight,": Goldberg, "Auburn Defense Does the Job," p. 16.

2 Our defense did its homework and did the job.: Goldberg, "Auburn Defense Does the Job," p. 16.

3 "If you're jumping off of a . . . the glory in everything you do.": Julie Kay, "Leap of Faith," *The Advocate*, Aug. 14, 2004, http://us.mg2.mail.yahoo.com/dc/launch?.gx=1&rand=62u6vmak9i5ru.

3 I never pray about winning, but I thank God when it happens.: Kay, "Leap of Faith."

4 "There were a lot of times . . . it did not look good,": Stewart Mandel, "Race to the End Zone," *Sports Illustrated Presents Auburn Tigers: Pride of the Plains* (New York City: Time, Inc., 2011), p. 27.

4 You feel good when they . . . defense in the country.: Mandel, "Race to the End Zone."

5 the only time all season Auburn fell behind: Clyde Bolton, *War Eagle* (Huntsville: The Strode Publishers, 1973), p. 218.

5 "Shug made a good speech in there,": Mark Murphy, *Game of My Life: Auburn* (Champaign IL: Sports Publishing L.L.C., 2007), p. 14.

5 He told his players they . . . a lot on the line here,": Mark Murphy, *Game of My Life: Auburn*, p. 15.

5 he was "way up over the punter.": Mark Murphy, *Game of My Life: Auburn*, p. 15.

5 "I believe that game was . . . they could win every game.: Mark Murphy, *Game of My Life: Auburn*, p. 15.

5 After [the State win] we said, 'By golly, we can win every game.': Mark Murphy, *Game of My Life: Auburn*, p. 15.

6 The Luck Stops Here.": Sally Jenkins, "Catch This!" *Sports Illustrated*, Oct. 24, 1994, p. 36.

6 "That is not a matter . . . belief in themselves, and inspired coaching.": Jenkins, p. 36.

6 "As for luck," . . . that Auburn couldn't win without it.": Jenkins, p. 36.

6 That wasn't a fluke. You can't call this luck.: Jenkins, p. 36.

7 "Everybody's tweeting about it . . . reporters called for interviews: "Auburn Ranked No. 1 in Latest BCS Rankings," *All In: Auburn's Run to the National Championship* (Cumming, GA: *Ledger-Enquirer*/TD Publishing, 2011), p. 77.

7 "It means a lot,": "Auburn Ranked No. 1," p. 76.

7 "We just had a team . . . week is another new week.": "Auburn Ranked No. 1," p. 77.

7 "You don't take [any]one lightly,": "Auburn Ranked No. 1," p. 77.

7   As a team, we don't . . . to get our fans excited.: "Auburn Ranked No. 1," p. 77.

8   their situation at running back . . . start of his junior year.: Ray Glier, *What It Means to Be a Tiger* (Chicago: Triumph Books, 2010), p. 147.

8   Playing golf with his coach . . . "You were wrong.": Glier, p. 147.

9   "Injured, exhausted, and exposed, . . . giving up 43 points and 566 yards.": Andy Bitter, "Tigers 'Refuse to Lose,'" *All In: Auburn's Run to the National Championship* (Cumming, GA: *Ledger-Enquirer*/TD Publishing, 2011), p. 60.

9   "oscillated between non-existent and passable.": Jay G. Tate, "'We Refuse to Lose,'" *All In: Auburn's Incredible Run to the National Championship* (Chicago: Triumph Books/*Montgomery Advertiser*, 2011), p. 73.

9   "Once we got that . . . of confidence out there.": Bitter, "Tigers 'Refuse to Lose,'" p. 60.

10   "It should be the goal," . . . expectations are there now.": Evan Woodbery, "Auburn's Chances Up in the Air," *All in to Win* (Birmingham: *The Birmingham News*, 2011), p. 60.

10   "the promise for this season is real.": Woodbery, "Auburn's Chances Up in the Air," p. 60.

10   "There are guys on our . . . that [is] extremely important.": Bill Bryant, "Tigers Are Deeper and More Experienced," *All in to Win* (Birmingham: *The Birmingham News*, 2011), p. 61.

10   the days of "having to go . . . non-stop" were over.: Bryant, "Tigers Are Deeper," p. 61.

10   Any time you have . . . there's a confidence there.: Bryant, "Tigers Are Deeper," p. 61.

11   Coaches insist that the time . . . from Jan. 1 to May 31,: Richard Scott, *An Inside Look at a Perfect Season* (Champaign, IL: Sports Publishing L.L.C., 2005), p. 6.

11   Yoxall resorted to "discretionary" . . . really kind of disappointed.": Scott, p. 7.

11   I was very concerned because we were behind where we needed to be.: Scott, p. 7.

12   "an ornery old guy" . . . ripped Roland's helmet off.: Glier, p. 185.

12   tackle Stacy Searels grabbed . . . you're not gonna play for me.": Glier, p. 187.

12   I wasn't taking his stuff that day.: Glier, p. 187.

13   "made the most difficult decision . . . for the team at quarterback.: Jay G. Tate, "Auburn's Burns Enjoys Life," *Montgomery Advertiser*, Aug. 17, 2010, https://secure.pqarchiver.com/montgomeryadvertiser/access/2118297881.

13   "I'd never caught a pass . . . threw me out there.": Tate, "Auburn's Burns Enjoys Life."

13   "He was a quarterback playing wide receiver,": Andy Bitter, "Auburn Football: Kodi Burns," *Ledger-Enquirer*, Aug. 23, 2010, http://www.ledger-enquirer.com/2010/08/23/1239684.

13   We wouldn't be the team we are today without Kodi setting the example.: Jay G. Tate, "Iron Bowl: Burns' Unselfishness," *Montgomery Advertiser*, Nov. 23, 2010, https://secure.pqarchiver.com/montgomeryadvertiser/sccess/2195168321.

14   During two-a-days prior . . . the incision from his hip to his knee: Chette Williams, *Hard Fighting Soldier* (Decatur, GA: Looking Glass Books, Inc., 2007), p. 164.

14   required one hundred stitches to repair.: "Steve Gandy," *The Sports Xchange*, Feb. 20, 2012, http://www.nfldraftscout.com/ratings/dsprofile.php?pyid=1697&draftyear=2009.

14   As Gandy recovered in . . . with strength coach Kevin Yoxall.: Williams, p. 164.

14   He also asked his teammates . . . to pray for healing.: Williams, pp. 164-65.

14   Team chaplain Chette Williams . . . for God's healing touch.: Williams, p. 165.

14   Whenever you've gone through . . . you need to protect him.: "Steve Gandy," *The Sports Xchange.*

15   "We're honored to be in the . . . playing for the championship.": Scott, p. 173.

15   A number of them regularly called . . . the 2004 team hadn't had.: Jon Solomon, "Finally in the Big Show," *All in to Win* (Birmingham: *The Birmingham News*, 2011), p. 44.

15   I reminded our guys all year how badly we wanted to play in '04.: Solomon, "Finally in the Big Show," p. 44.

16   The Auburn coaches invited Downs . . . afraid of the contact,": Jon Johnson, "Former HA Player Watson Downs Performs Well for Auburn," *Dothan Eagle*, Nov. 10, 2010, http://www2.dothaneagle.com/sports/2010/nov/10.

16   The omnipresent TV cameras . . . when I hit him,': Johnson, "Former HA Player."

189

16   You're just grateful for . . . just being on the team.: Johnson, 'Former HA Player."

17   If there is a better 1950s . . . never heard it.": J. Henderson, "Genealogy of Nick-name," *The War Eagle Reader*, Sept. 11, 2007, http://thewareaglereader.wordpress.com/2007/09/11.

17   an Alabama graduate in town . . .one of his last scholarships.: Bolton, p. 224.

17   The moniker was slapped . . . fondness for Zeke Bratkowski,: Henderson, "Genealogy of a Nickname."

17   "At first I missed playing . . . I just wanted to play.": Bolton, p. 224.

17   I guess that name will stick . . . Nobody does but my mother.: Bolton, p. 222.

18   The Rebs loaded the line . . . Newton wherever he went.: Jay G. Tate, "Tigers Trump 'Trap Game,'" *All In: Auburn's Incredible Run to the National Championship* (Chicago: Triumph Books/Montgomery Advertiser, 2011) p. 89.

18   Tonight they did a nice . . . had to work other avenues.: Charles Goldberg, "Auburn Beats Ole Miss," *All in to Win* (Birmingham: *The Birmingham News*, 2011), p. 112.

19   "got stuck with the nastiest . . . he was "basically a starter.": Josh Moon, "Tigers Saved by Bell," *Montgomery Advertiser*, Nov. 30, 2010, https://secure.pqarchiver.com/montgomeryadvertiser/access/2200659421.

19   Ted Roof called for Bell . . . him to the ground.: Moon, "Tigers Saved by Bell."

19   appeared to have a touchdown. . . . ripped through two blockers,: Moon, "Tigers Saved by Bell."

19   I took it personal. I really did.: Moon, "Tigers Saved by Bell."

20   Jordan was on the varsity . . . Get in there.": Rich Donnell, *Shug* (Montgomery: Owl Bay Publishers, 1993), p. 55.

20   "every inning was two outs . . . men left on base.": Donnell, p. 55.

20   Florida smacked eleven hits . . . Floridans on the basepath.": Donnell, p. 55.

20   Florida loaded the bases in the ninth . . . for the final out.: Donnell, pp. 55-56.

20   I was an atrocious pitcher.: Donnell, p. 56.

21   If the Tigers ever had . . . to be a good time for it.": Scott, p. 146.

21   "The one thing about this . . . "They'll enjoy going to Tuscaloosa.": Scott, p. 145.

21   The Tiger offense produced . . . its first three possessions.: Scott, p. 146.

21   "The kids were relatively calm," . . . to get the offense moving.: Scott, p. 147.

21   The Tigers behaved as . . . knew just what to do.: Scott, p. 146.

22   He was so sure he . . . just not messing up,": Jay G. Tate, "Auburn's Mosley Makes Best of Opportunity," *Montgomery Advertiser*, Sept. 13, 2010, https://secure.pq archiver.com/montgomeryadvertiser/access/2136528671.

22   His eyes were big and stuff.: Tate, "Auburn's Mosley Makes Best of Opportunity."

23   You cannot overestimate the . . . stadium on our program.: Landon Thomas, *The SEC Team of the '80s: Auburn Football 1980-1989* (Woodstock, GA: Tiger Publishing, 2004), p. 256.

24   "Hey, man," he said, "you . . .gonna help us win it.": Austin Murphy, ""On the Biggest Stage, New Stars Emerged," *Sports Illustrated Presents Auburn Tigers: Pride of the Plains* (New York City: Time, Inc., 2011), p. 52.

25   For fleeting minutes, Auburn . . . as it had never been tested before.": Phillip Marshall, *The Auburn Experience* (Auburn: Phillip Marshall, 2004), p. 291.

25   She hyperextended both knees so . . .time for me to be finished.": Marshall, p. 291.

25   It's kind of like God's . . . but it's given to you.: Marshall, p. 292.

26   Turnovers are strange things. Sometimes they come in bunches.: Evan Woodbery, "4th Quarter Turnovers Put Tigers on Top," *All in to Win* (Birmingham: *The Birmingham News*, 2011), p. 82.

27   Rogers honestly didn't think he would win the Thorpe Award.: Scott, p. 66.

27   "Carlos is a lock-down . . . half of the field by himself,": Scott, p. 68.

27   "No one would throw at him . . . general direction the whole year.": Scott, p. 69.

27   "The quarterbacks would just turn and look the other way,": Scott, p. 69.

27   he would leave his . . . he was an open receiver.: Scott, p. 69.

28   He was "an introspective . . . speech is going to say.": Jay G. Tate, "Auburn Football: Ziemba's Speech Credited in AU's Drive Toward Win," *Montgomery Advertiser*, Oct. 13, 2010, https://secure.pqarchiver.com/mongtomeryadvertiser/access/2161377811.

28   "began to feel the fire." . . . It wasn't a big deal.": Tate, "Ziemba's Speech Credited."

TIGERS

28   Quarterback Cam Newton had . . . lay with his left tackle.: Tate, "Ziemba's Speech Credited."

28   What was new to . . . was Lee Ziemba's pep talk.: Tate, "Ziemba's Speech Credited."

29   The players were "hoodlums," . . . "mental idleness to the participant.": Bolton, 59.

29   In 1897, the Birmingham News . . . greater menace to human life.": Bolton, p. 57.

29   In 1903, L.S. Boyd, an Auburn . . . the game at his alma mater.: Bolton, p. 58.

29   In calling for the Alabama . . . worthless system of college athletics.; Bolton, p. 59.

29   since athletics had begun at Auburn . . . sober-mindedness of the olden time.": Bolton, pp. 60-61.

29   The modern college student has . . . as an intelligent billy-goat.: Bolton, p. 60.

30   "Somebody told somebody else . . . Toomer's Corner in celebration.: Mark McCarter, "Auburn's 1957 National Championship Came From Nowhere," *The Huntsville Times*, Jan. 6, 2011, http://www.al.com/sports/index.ssf/2011/01/auburn_1957_national_champions.html.

30   Buster Gross, a student coach . . . the Tigers on Dec. 10.: Jimmy Smothers, "Gross Recalls Being Part of Auburn's '57 Title Team," *Gadsden Times*, Jan. 9, 2011, http://www.gadsdentimes.com/article/20110109/news/110109839?p=4&tc=pg.

30   "no one fretted much about . . . inside the Tiger football team.": McCarter, "Auburn's 1957 National Championship Came from Nowhere."

30   "We knew the '57 . . . the end of the season.": Smothers, "Gross Recalls Being Part."

30   Head coach Shug Jordan didn't . . . of being a national champion.": McCarter, "Auburn's 1957 National Championship Came from Nowhere."

30   They announced [the national . . . for a big dinner.": Smothers, "Gross Recalls Being Part."

31   "We were on the verge of being terrible.": Austin Murphy, "Iron Giants," *Sports Illustrated Presents Auburn Tigers: Pride of the Plains* (New York City: Time, Inc., 2011), p. 35.

31   Writer Austin Murphy described Auburn's play in the final 30 minutes as "astonishing.": Austin Murphy, "Iron Giants," p. 36.

31   We know our offense . . . a quarter, no problem.: Austin Murphy, "Iron Giants," p. 36.

32   "alarmingly bad." . . . minutes into the second quarter.: Evan Woodbery, "A Heart-Stopping Win," *All in to Win* (Birmingham: *The Birmingham News*, 2011), p. 76.

32   Head coach Gene Chizik insisted . . . "from bumbling to brilliant.": Woodbery, "A Heart-Stopping Win," p. 76.

32   players running to the . . . to make even more noise.: Woodbery, "A Heart-Stopping Win," p. 76.

32   the refs signalled a . . . double-clutching the snap.: Woodbery, "A Heart-Stopping Win," p. 76.

33   Lorino's dad put an end . . . 12:01 a.m. the signing began.: Mark Murphy, *Game of My Life*, p. 128.

33   It was like espionage, . . . of sight and hidden.: Mark Murphy, *Game of My Life*, p. 128.

34   Tim Carter caught a pass . . . sideline later in the game.: Ivan Maisel and Kelly Whiteside, *A War in Dixie* (New York City: HarperCollins Publishers, 2001), p. 177.

35   The combination of a perfect . . . Washington was upset.": Jay G. Tate, "AU's Washington Makes an Impact on Special Teams," *Montgomery Advertiser*, Nov. 5, 2010, https://secure.pqarchiver.com/montgomeryadvertiser/access/2180801301.

35   "penchant for assignment errors . . . a newfound confidence.: Tate, "AU's Washington Makes an Impact."

35   He wanted the . . . throw at him again.: Tate, "AU's Washington Makes an Impact."

35   "I was happy they . . . hero: 10 minutes.": Tate, "AU's Washington Makes an Impact."

35   I had to redeem . . . let the team down.: Tate, "AU's Washington Makes an Impact."

36   "more unblockable than any defensive lineman in the nation.": Lars Anderson, "Making the Man," *Sports Illustrated Presents Auburn Tigers: Pride of the Plains* (New York City: Time, Inc., 2011) p. 65.

36   Fairley played with a mean . . . is to get that quarterback." Anderson, "Making the Man," p. 67.

36   "immediately became Copiah-Lincoln's most dominating player.": Anderson, "Making the Man," p. 66.

36   Only thirty minutes after his . . . in here and stay focused,": Anderson, "Making the Man," p. 66.

36   The whole experience . . . It changed his life.: Anderson, "Making the Man," p. 66.

37   "LSU is always in the back of your mind,": Scott, p. 23.

37   "They beat us in about . . . focused on this game,": Scott, p. 22.

37   We've been trying hard not to let them look ahead.: Scott, p. 22.

38   "the most accomplished golfer in Auburn history, male or female.": Marshall, p. 262.

38   Troche started playing golf when . . . to live with relatives.: Marshall, p. 262.

38   Troche spoke Spanish and German . . . know what I was studying.": Marshall, p. 262.

38   She played on the boys golf team . . . "It would be 100 boys and me.": Marshall, p. 262.

38   It was a good challenge and made . . . work harder to beat the guys.: Marshall, p. 262.

39   At the midpoint of the . . . put four quarters together?": Evan Woodbery, "Wildcats on the Run," *All in to Win* (Birmingham: *The Birmingham News*, 2011), p. 94.

39   "made Kentucky defenders look . . . an attention-grabbing blowout.": Woodbery, "Wildcats on the Run," p. 94.

39   We are finding interesting ways to end the games.: Andy Ritter, "Tigers Keep Finding Ways to Win," *All In* (Cumming, GA: *The Ledger-Enquirer*/TD Publishing, 2011), p. 52.

40   Today was the first step toward winning the SEC championship.": Thomas, p. 95.

40   Head coach Pat Dye put his . . . fight-for-your-life situation,": Thomas, p. 93.

40   cut up the middle . . . final block from Jimmie Warren: Thomas, p. 93.

41   Prior to the 2011 Chick- . . . after their first touchdown.: Evan Woodbery, "Auburn's Special Teams Help Seal Chick-Fil-A Bowl Win," al.com, Dec. 31, 2011, http://www.al.com/sports/index.ssf.2011/12.

41   when the offense scored, . . . "I forgot,": Woodbery, "Auburn's Special Teams."

41   the assistants jogged Chizik's . . . before pouncing on it.: Woodbery, "Auburn's Special Teams."

41   I think we're undefeated on that onside kick.: Woodbery, "Auburn's Special Teams."

42   "Auburn's perfect record belied a season of gritty, grinding comebacks.": Andy Staples, "Up in the Air," *Sports Illustrated Presents Auburn Tigers: Pride of the Plains* (New York City: Time, Inc., 2011), p. 39.

42   "it seemed as if . . . granted some breathing room.": Staples, "Up in the Air," p. 39.

42   We've been in that situation . . . is the key to success.: Evan Woodbery, "Rematch in Atlanta," *All in to Win* (Birmingham: *The Birmingham News*, 2011), p. 40.

43   After giving its fans heart palpitations for three straight weeks,": Andy Ritter, "Blowout of Louisiana-Monroe," *All In: Auburn's Run to the National Championship* (Cumming, GA: *Ledger-Enquirer*/TD Publishing, 2011), p. 46.

43   "It's hard to keep from watching,": Bill Bryant, "Come-From-Behind Tigers," *All in to Win* (Birmingham: *The Birmingham News*, 2011), p. 85.

43   "it's a God thing.": Woodbery, "A Heart-Stopping Win," p. 76.

43   The coaches found sixty-eight . . . prudent on how we proceed,": Ritter, "Blowout of Louisiana-Monroe," p. 46.

43   the coaches didn't call . . . averaging 19 carries a game.: Jon Solomon, "Can They Keep the Big Mo?" *All in to Win* (Birmingham: *The Birmingham News*, 2011), p. 90.

43   Our plan was to keep [Cam Newton] from running the ball.: Evan Woodbery, "A Win with Style," *All in to Win* (Birmingham: *The Birmingham News*, 2011), p. 88.

44   "rumbled ominously to the brink of the Auburn goal.": Wayne Hester, *Where Tradition Began* (Birmingham, Seacoast Publishing/*The Birmingham News*, 1991), p. 60.

44   "I was confident that it . . . saw it going through there.": Hester, p. 60.

44   It was the first one . . . come at a better time.: Hester, p. 60.

45   This is one they'll . . . another 75 years from now.": Mark McCarter, "The Comeback," *All in to Win* (Birmingham: *The Birmingham News*, 2011), p. 133.

45   "This is probably the best . . . go down in history.": Mark McCarter, "The Comeback," p. 133.

45   the Tigers did some talking . . . Just go out and do it.": Don Kausler Jr., "Come-From-Behind Slugfest Puts Tide Under," *All in to Win* (Birmingham: *The Birmingham News*, 2011), p. 130.

45   "I really didn't think . . . great things happen.": Kausler, "Come-From-Behind Slugfest," p. 130.

45 If makes me feel fast.: Kausler, "Come-From-Behind Slugfest," p. 130.
46 The coaches decided they needed . . . practicing it all week.: Scott, p. 86.
46 "It worked sometime, but . . . down the sideline.: Scott, p. 86.
46 I was just hoping and praying it would work.: Scott, p. 86.
47 On Feb. 8, 2011, the Montgomery Quarterback . . . watch him receive his trophy.":
     Mike Tankersley, "Auburn's Trench Stars Bask in Title," *Montgomery Advertiser*,
     Feb. 9, 2011. https://secure.pqarchiver.com/montgomeryadvertiser/access/
     2272893491.html.
47 As soon as the two . . . and they watched you.": Tankersley, "Auburn's Trench Stars
     Bask in Title."
47 It's sinking in more and more every day.: Tankersley, "Auburn's Trench Stars Bask in
     Title."
48 "The 2010 team was a far . . . Alabama had $2.: "AU's Championship Warms Housel's
     Heart," *Montgomery Advertiser*, Sept. 10, 2011, http://pqasb.pqarchiver.com/
     montgomeryadvertiser/access/2451832001.html.
49 "We were not happy about it,": Donnell, p. 123.
49 "We were all down," . . . and jackets they would be getting.: Donnell, p. 123-24.
49 An assistant coach then dropped . . . bowl officials had told him.: Donnell, p. 124.
49 He then met with the team . . . receive their watches and jackets.: Donnell, p. 125.
50 This is the big time, guys.": George Schroeder, "The Visionary, "*Sports Illustrated
     Presents Auburn Tigers: Pride of the Plains* (New York City: Time, Inc., 2011), p. 69.
50 Sitting high in the stands. . . pronouncement to his players.: Schroeder, "The Vision-
     ary," p. 69.
50 "It was a little overwhelming,": Schroeder, "The Visionary," p. 69.
50 The head coach figured . . . he'd better not blow it.": Schroeder, "The Visionary," p. 69.
50 He lived in a trailer . . . He was always doodling,": Schroeder, "The Visionary," p. 70.
50 "I thought I'd never . . . never get a chance again.": Schroeder, "The Visionary," p. 71.
50 ran a scheme nearly identical to what that Hughes team did in 1994.: Schroeder, "The
     Visionary," p. 70.
50 "It's the opposite end . . . be coaching at college.": Schroeder, "The Visionary," p. 71.
50 God's been so good to me, and I don't know why.: Schroeder, "The Visionary," p. 71.
51 He simply showed up one day . . . if he could play.: Mark McCarter, "Auburn's
     Quindarius Carr Nearing End of 'Blessed' Career," *The Huntsville Times*, Nov.
     25, 2011, http://www.al.com/sports/index.ssf/2011/11.
51 "rock bottom" because of . . . view of "sheer perfection": McCarter, "Auburn's
     Quindarius Carr."
51 "I feel good about . . . for us out there,": McCarter, "Auburn's Quindarius Carr."
51 "I've had an awesome time . . . has been a blessing.": McCarter, "Auburn's Quindarius
     Carr."
52 On Wednesday night before . . . a called "Hard Fighting Soldier.": Williams, p. 145.
52 Friday night in Knoxville, toward . . . hymn again by request.: Williams, pp. 145-46.
52 this time, everyone joined in. . . . onto the field for the game.: Williams, p. 146.
52 Then in the locker room after . . . the players sang again.: Williams, pp. 146-47.
52 The "locker room became a . . . joyously witnessing for Christ.: Williams, p. 147.
52 God had transformed us into witnesses.: Williams, p. 147.
53 "Everyone wants the ball . . . do what I can with it.": Jay G. Tate, "Lutzenkirchen's
     Patience Paying Off with New Role," *Montgomery Advertiser*, Sept. 30, 2010,
     https://secure.pqarchiver.com/montgomeryadvertiser/access/2150514211.
53 Wideout Emory Blake described . . . "a tough catch.": Tate, "Lutzenkirchen's Patience
     Paying Off."
53 I just had to be . . . to get some touches.: Tate, "Lutzenkirchen's Patience Paying Off."
54 Freeman hopped up at once; . . . keeping up with each other,: Ron Higgins, "A
     Strange But Fitting Friendship," *SECNation*, Oct. 28, 1010, http://www.sec
     digitalnetwork.com/SECNation/SECTraditions/tabid/1073/Article/214902.
54 It is kind of weird, . . . saved my life.: Higgins, "A Strange But Fitting Friendship."
55 the stiffest penalty the NCAA had ever handed out.: Ed Hinton, "Shug's Time
     to Shine," *Sports Illustrated Presents Auburn Tigers: Pride of the Plains* (New
     York City: Time, Inc., 2011), p. 74.
55 Jordan was so concerned . . . to scout the Sooners.: Paul Hemphill,

"Our First Time," *Auburn Magazine*, Fall 2007, p. 23.

55   Jordan kicked both his . . . tends to draw men together.": Hemphill, p. 23.

55   Unless Coach Ralph 'Shug' . . . slow-footed and dim-witted.: Hemphill, p. 24.

56   Auburn believes it's on the cusp of something great.: Jay G. Tate, "Newton's Law," *Montgomery Advertiser*, Aug. 28, 1010, https://secure.pqarchiver.com/montgom eryadvertiser/access/2124632701.

56   "We feel like we're not being mentioned as we should be,": Tate, "Newton's Law."

56   offensive coordinator Gus Malzahn . . . than it was in 2009.: Tate, "Newton's Law."

56   "The only real weaknesses [. . . ones we create ourselves.": Tate, "Newton's Law."

56   I guess if you win games, you'll silence all the critics.: Tate, "Newton's Law."

57   Discussions about whether the . . . had no such intentions.: Scott, p. 31.

57   The school cancelled classes and students ran for home.: Scott, p. 31.

57   the team moved into a downtown hotel.: Scott, p. 32.

57   "We had to meet something . . . could practice at a time.: Scott, p. 32.

57   "Our preparation from a . . . everything I've ever preached,": Scott, p. 33.

57   You can't control the weather, so we just have to know how to adjust.: Scott, p. 32.

58   They tweaked the schemes on . . . known nothing but success.: Josh Moon, "Turning Point," *Montgomery Advertiser*, Nov. 27, 2010, https://secure.pqarchiver.com/montgomeryadvertiser/access/2198638751.

58   "We wanted (that opening . . . could keep it rolling.": Moon, "Turning Point."

58   Offensive coordinator Gus . . . only the week before.: Moon, "Turning Point."

58   That was a big thing we talked about -- having early success.: Moon, "Turning Point."

59   "one lousy stop": Austin Murphy, "On the Biggest Stage," p. 42.

59   "a sequence more surreal . . . unveiled for the occasion.": Austin Murphy, "On the Biggest Stage," p. 44.

59   "Play came to a stop. The Ducks' defense relaxed.": Austin Murphy, "On the Biggest Stage," p. 44.

59   only to hear his coaches . . . screaming "Run!" and "Go!": Bill Bryant, "True Freshman Dyer Is Big Play-Maker," *All in to Win* (Birmingham: *The Birmingham News*, 2011), p. 28.

59   "At the time I . . . waiting to hear a whistle.": Bryant, "True Freshman Dyer," p. 28.

59   [Michael Dyer] did a great . . . He made a play.: Bryant, "True Freshman Dyer," p. 28.

60   Gardner started playing when he . . . facing the other way,": Marshall, p. 254.

60   He grew up in an Auburn family . . . That's why we won.": Marshall, p. 255.

60   Shortly before the tournament, he . . . had surgery on the finger.: Marshall, p. 255.

60   To this day, I can tell you if it's going to rain.: Marshall, p. 255.

61   "We've got one shot. Let's get it done,": Scott, p. 36.

61   its 192nd consecutive extra . . . a PAT kick since 1999.: Scott, p. 38.

61   The snapper rolled the ball . . . in the pit of my stomach,": Scott, p. 38.

61   "due to a new and relatively . . . again rolled back to Rives.: Scott, pp. 38-39.

61   Sometimes you just have to have lucky things go your way.: Scott, p. 39.

62   outstanding defense, excellent kicking, no mistakes: Donnell, p. 142.

62   "we had too many . . . people we were counting on.": Donnell, p. 135.

62   "You don't get fat playing . . . made them run a lap.: Donnell, p. 139.

62   I think God made it simple. Just accept Him and believe.: Jim & Julie S. Bettinger, *The Book of Bowden* (Nashville: TowleHouse Publishing, 2001), p. 47.

63   He developed a reputation . . . going hard on every play,": Jay G. Tate, "No Pain, No Gain," *Montgomery Advertiser*, Sept. 23, 2010, https://secure.pqarchiver.com/montgomeryadvertiser/access/2144737041.

63   Bynes was being hailed . . . unquestioned leader" of the team.: Chris Low, "Josh Bynes Has Been Auburn's Rock," *College Football Nation Blog*, Jan. 8, 2011, http://espn.go.com/blog/ncfnation/post/_/id/37694.

63   Minutes before he was to . . . his teammates' amusement).: Evan Woodbery, "Auburn Linebacker Josh Bynes," *al.com*, July 23, 2010, http://www.al.com/sports/index.ssf/2010/07/josh_bynes_blog_entry.html.

63   He's taken a load on . . . It's the best thing.: Jay G. Tate, "Auburn Notebook: Backup Jessel Curry," *Montgomery Advertiser*, Sept. 23, 2010, https://secure.pqarchiver.com/montgomeryadvertiser/access/2144737031.

64   On a chilly January night . . . first steps toward redemption.: Lars Anderson,

"Tiger Burning Bright," *Sports Illustrated Presents Auburn Tigers: Pride of the Plains* (New York City: Time, Inc., 2011), p. 59.

64   "hoping to become the next Tim Tebow.": Anderson, "Tiger Burning Bright," p. 60.

64   He insisted he had . . . immediately decided to transfer.: Anderson, "Tiger Burning Bright," p. 61.

64   Exhausted, scared, and not wanting . . . place that would save him.": Anderson, "Tiger Burning Bright," p. 59.

64   "I'm an example of why people deserve second chances,": Anderson, "Tiger Burning Bright," p. 60.

64   I've grown so much as . . . my time in Brenham.: Anderson, "Tiger Burning Bright," p. 60.

65   Friday night before Saturday's . . . They were gone -- swept away.: Williams, p. 158.

65   ordinarily one of the most . . . of a freshman's life.: Williams, p. 156.

65   As a redshirt, Horton met . . . met the bus at the stadium.: Williams, p. 158.

65   Head coach Tommy Tuberville was the first . . . and cried with him.: Williams, p. 158.

65   But then the band struck up . . . through the cheering crowd : Williams, pp. 158-59.

65   That's when something unexpected . . . was at that Tiger Walk.": Williams, p. 159.

65   The following Sunday, Horton . . . the voices of his brothers.: Williams, p. 160.

65   I felt like I was walking to the light.: Williams, p. 159.

66   a time when head coach . . . get your ankles taped.": Glier, p. 181.

66   "It was brutal," . . . I looked like Frankenstein,": Glier, p. 182.

66   the Tigers didn't recruit him; . . . in football and baseball,": Glier, p. 182.

66   I had to go prove myself again and make them regret not recruiting me.: Glier, p.183.

67   "a major disaipointment," . . . meeting of the whole team.: Jon Solomon, "Chizik to Offense," *All in to Win* (Birmingham: *The Birmingham News*, 2011), p. 78.

67   While Auburn led the . . . out of the pocket.: Solomon, "Chizik to Offense," p. 78.

67   Against Clemson, the Tigers . . . yards or less.: Solomon, "Chizik to Offense," p. 79.

67   Chizik said the line . . . are embarrassed.": Solomon, "Chizik to Offense," p. 78.

67   You definitely won't hear . . . I'll guarantee that.: Solomon, "Chizik to Offense," p. 79.

68   Junior fullback Greg Pratt, slated . . . in the best shape possible.: Thomas, p. 90.

68   he made two practice runs without any problem.: Marshall, p. 24.

68   He passed the physical given to all the players that morning.: Thomas, p. 90.

68   The afternoon of the test . . . him on the last one.: Marshall, p. 24.

68   On the last lap, Hallman . . . and helped him finish.: Thomas, p. 90.

68   "I'd collapsed a couple of . . . brought them the awful news: Marshall, p. 24.

68   Dye led his team in prayer . . . the high goals they all had.: Thomas, p. 90.

68   That tragedy was there all year.: Marshall, p. 24.

69   "In the first quarter, . . . never played football before.": Jay G. Tate, "Auburn Atlanta Bound," *All In: Auburn's Incredible Run to the National Championship* (Chicago: Triumph Books/*Montgomery Advertiser*, 2011), p. 99.

69   "We had to settle down,": Tate, "Auburn Atlanta Bound," p. 99.

69   "build long, sustained drives . . . the brink of exhaustion.": Tate, "Auburn Atlanta Bound," p. 101

69   "changed the game's dynamic": Tate, "Auburn Atlanta Bound," p. 101.

69   In reviewing film of the . . . blocking formation too early.: Tate, "Auburn Atlanta Bound, pp. 99, 101.

69   "That was huge because . . a drive from them,": Tate, "Auburn Atlanta Bound," p. 101.

69   [The onside kick] swung the momentum in the second half.: Charles Goldberg, "Chizik and His Tigers Claim SEC West Title," *All in to Win* (Birmingham: *The Birmingham News*, 2011), p. 126.

70   "devastating. Guys just couldn't hit it.": Marshall, p. 224.

70   during that time off, . . . the weapon that made his career.: Marshall, p. 224.

70   "I wouldn't trade it for the world,": Marshall, p. 225.

70   When he left Auburn, he . . . You don't listen like you should.": Marshall, p. 225.

70   Looking back, I probably . . . as well as I should have.: Marshall, p. 225.

71   That's when Gran, the running . . . would come flying out,: Scott, p. 110.

71   "If we fumble and they get . . . to do to win the game,": Scott, p. 111.

71   We got the ball, scattered like . . . and ran the ball out to the 22-yard line.: Scott, p. 111.

195

72 in the BCS national title . . . "because they had patience.": Tommy Hicks, "Tigers' Patience, Not Speed, Seals BCS Win," *All in to Win* (Birmingham: *The Birmingham News*, 2011), p. 21.

72 They would pound the . . . or run to the corners.: Hicks, "Tigers' Patience," p. 21.

72 "We just tried to move . . . some time off the clock,": Hicks, "Tigers' Patience," p. 21.

72 "We just had to go with the flow, one play at a time,": Hicks, "Tigers' Patience," p. 21.

72 Just getting in field goal . . . any time on the clock.: Hicks, "Tigers' Patience," p. 21.

73 Auburn might have won the football . . . at that instant.": Hester, p. 58.

73 In September, Jordan simply . . . and told Nix, "You're it.": Hester, p. 59.

73 "42,000 people shivering under . . . to see what [Nix[would do.": Hester, p. 58.

73 Nix studied the down marker for . . . It had been discarded: Hester, p. 58.

73 Thirty-seven, H, Belly had . . . found the answer for the moment.: Hester, p. 58.

74 Following Auburn's 56-17 demolition . . . to capture the moment.: Brad Zimanek, "Montgomery Family Enjoying Auburn's Ride to National Title Game," *Montgomery Advertiser*, Jan. 5, 2011, https://secure.pqarchiver.com/montgomery advertiser/access/2229892471.

74 This opportunity is . . . couldn't be happier,": Zimanek, "Montgomery Family."

74 giving up football became . . . t some point.: Zimanek, "Montgomery Family."

74 With us it starts with family and God.: Zimanek, "Montgomery Family."

75 "I'd say I had some . . . making it as I did.": Marshall, p. 100.

75 "I was actually the first . . . compared to human life.": Marshall, p. 99.

76 It came on a second-and . . . after a two-yard gain.: Jay G. Tate, "Pile-Moving Play in LSU Contest," *Montgomery Advertiser*, Oct. 28, 2010, https://secure.pqarchiver. com/montgomeryadvertiser/access/2174413861.

76 Dyer kept driving his legs, . . . when we were doing it,": Tate, "Pile-Moving Play."

76 As we started to . . . something like no other.: Tate, "Pile-Moving Play."

76 the play the TV announcer called 'a scrum': Tate, "Pile-Moving Play."

77 They left tight end Philip Lutzenkirchen all alone,": Jay G. Tate, "(23) Auburn 42, Utah State 38 -- AU-spicious Start: Tigers Avoid Upset Bid," *Montgomery Advertiser*, Sept. 4, 2011. https://secure.pqarchiver.com/montgomeryadvertiser/ access/2442449391.html.

77 The team's top kickers, . . . to get it 10 yards.": Tate, "(23) Auburn 42, Utah State 38."

78 resulting in "season-wrecking derailings." . . . the exstence of The Hawg Hex.: Van Allen Plexico and John Ringer, *Season of Our Dreams* (White Rocket Books, 2011), p. 51.

78 The Hex "was in full effect": Plexico and Ringer, p. 52.

78 The Hawg Hex then "bloomed . . . of 2001 and 2002": Plexico and Ringer, p. 52.

78 While the Hawg Hex is . . . enough to slow down CamZilla.: Plexico and Ringer, p. 57.

79 He had played his senior year . . . the kid had talent.: Jay G. Tate, "Auburn's Sullen Gets Svelte," *Montgomery Advertiser*, Aug. 7, 2010, https://secure.pqarchiver. com/montgomery/advertiser/access/2103123821.html.

79 "I wish I could have . . . than he had ever been.: Tate, "Auburn's Sullen Gets Svelte."

79 It was just something I had to deal with.: Tate, "Auburn's Sullen Gets Svelte."

80 Those lenses intrigued Beckwith . . . feel 'em and grab 'em.": Bolton, pp. 202-03.

80 "We got five or six . . . Auburn jersey, he grabbed it.": Bolton, p. 203.

80 I first sold him to the Associated Press.: Bolton, p. 202.

81 "perhaps the program's . . . player in a generation.": Jay G. Tate, "New Auburn QB Newton Lays Down Law," *All In: Auburn's Incredible Run to the National Championship* (Chicago: Triumph Books/*Montgomery Advertiser*, 2011), p. 37.

81 "all the hype surrounding Cam . . . even better than advertised.": Randy Kennedy, "Newton Lives Up to the Hype," *All in to Win* (Birmingham: *The Birmingham News*, 2011), p. 67.

81 Being his first football . . . of what he did.: Andy Bitter, "Tigers' New Quarterback Cam Newton Lives Up to Hype," *All In: Auburn's Run to the National Championship* (Cumming, GA: *Ledger-Enquirer*/TD Publishing, 2011), p. 14.

82 "the largest and loudest stadium they would face all season.": Scott, p. 59.

82 "I don't think it serves . . . takes a lot more concentration.: Scott, p. 59.

82 Offensive coordinator Al Borges . . . changing plays at the line.: Scott, p. 61.

82 "Coming into a place like Tennessee, . . . out of the game" early on.:

Scott, p. 65.

82 The Auburn tailback hit . . . the Volunteer's helmet flew off: Scott, p. 63.

82 all that deafening noise had been replaced by "a hushed gloom.": Scott, p. 65.

82 Loud is loud. Anywhere you go, it's loud.: Scott, p. 59.

83 "chest-bumping, towel-waving dynamo,": John Zenor, "Auburn's Towel-Waving Trooper Taylor Keeps Things Loose," *GoVolsXtra*, Jan. 9, 2011, http://www.go volsxtra.com/news/2011/jan/09.

83 "players' big brother on . . . made Newton do his over.: Zenor, "Auburn's Towel-Waving Trooper."

83 he has kept hanging off . . . he didn't knock me down.": Zenor, "Auburn's Towel-Waving Trooper."

83 he daily flipped a piece . . . deep snapper Josh Harris.: Zenor, "Auburn's Towel-Waving Trooper."

83 Football's a game, . . . fun out of the game.: Zenor, "Auburn's Towel-Waving Trooper."

84 the superstitions "piled up to ridiculous proportions": Josh Moon, "Ziemba's Superstitions Take the Cake," *Montgomery Advertiser*, Jan. 9, 2011, https://secure.pqarchiver.com/montgomeryadvertiser/access/2233186191.

84 Ziemba, however, always . . . kept on winning,: Moon, "Ziemba's Superstitions.'

84 wideout Emory Blake's . . . on his right arm: Moon, "Ziemba's Superstitions."

84 It's disgusting, really . . . that's what it is.: Moon, "Ziemba's Superstitions."

85 "My dream was always baseball," . . . what I was best at.": Mark Murphy, *Game of My Life: Auburn*, p. 21.

85 Campbell was indeed playing that big . . . she didn't get mad at me.": Mark Murphy, *Game of My Life: Auburn*, p. 21.

86 they "survived" it.: "Auburn Came Back," *The Auburn Villager*, Jan 27, 2011, p. 6.

86 "We've got a lot of guys on this team that are relentless.": Auburn Came Back," p. 6.

86 "Auburn didn't seem tired. It seemed tough.": Jay G. Tate, "Comeback Tigers Do It Again," *All In: Auburn's Incredible Run to the National Championship* (Chicago: Triumph Books/ *Montgomery Advertiser*, 2011), p. 59.

86 He knew beforehand that . . . as the game went along,": "Auburn Came Back," p. 6.

86 "These guys are scratching, . . . to win every week,": "Auburn Came Back," p. 6.

86 Never count us out. We're never going to stop playing football.: Tate, "Comeback Tigers," p. 57.

87 He had grown up in a . . . about his father's deserting him.: Williams, p. 140.

87 Williams told the junior . . . at his grandmother's house.: Williams, p. 141.

87 They sat on the front . . . lasting relationship were disappointed.: Williams, p. 142.

87 That September during a team . . . and to unify the team.: Williams, p. 143.

87 It wasn't about me or my dad. . . . understand why God has us here.: Williams, p. 142.

88 "will be replayed for eternity in Iron Bowl circles.": Andy Bitter, "Tight End Lutzenkirchen Dances into Spotlight," *All In: Auburn's Run to the National Championship* (Cumming, GA: *Ledger-Enquirer*/TD Publishing, 2011), p. 106.

88 Praying he wouldn't drop it,: Bitter, "Tight End Lutzenkirchen Dances," p. 106.

88 Lutzenkirchn "waltzed toward the . . . from his teammates and friends.: Bitter, "Tight End Lutzenkirchen Dances," p. 106."

88 I hope it doesn't. I really hope it doesn't.: Bitter, "Tight End Lutzenkirchen Dances," p. 106."

89 It's just my job to catch it when they throw it to me.": Chris White, "Wide Receiver Darvin Adams Sets SEC Championship Game Record," *All In: Auburn's Run to the National Championship* (Cumming, GA: *Ledger-Enquirer*/TD Publishing, 2011), p. 125.

89 Adams was well . . . sas a blocker.: White, "Wide Receiver Darvin Adams," p. 125.

89 I was just trying to make my catches.: White, "Wide Receiver Darvin Adams," p. 125.

90 only after the wires were buried . . . late 1970s or early 1980s.: Mike Szvetitz, "Final Roll Celebrates Toomer's Corner Past," *oanow.com*, April 20, 2013, http://www. oanow.com/news/toomers_oaks/article.

90 "This is kind of going back" to the original tradition,: Kristen Oliver, "'New' Toomer's Corner Will Blend Past and Present Traditions," *oanow.com*, April 20, 2013, http://www.oanow.com/news/toomers_oaks/ article.

MORE AUBURN

90 "Traditions change. . . . more than two oak trees.": Szvetitz, "Final Roll Celebrates."

90 Something doesn't have to be old to be a tradition.: "Auburn Fans Roll Toomer's Corner after Spring Game," *SI.com*, April 21, 2013, http://sportsillustrated.cnnc.om/college-football-news/20130421/auburn-toomers-corner.

91 What he didn't have was . . . no offers came his way.: Joel A. Erickson, "Cameron Artis-Payne's Long, Winding Road," *al.com*, April 18, 2013, http://www.al.com/auburnfootball/index.ssf/2013/04.

91 He turned 20 living at home, working out,: Erickson, "Cameron Artis-Payne's Long, Winding Road."

91 In a casual conversation, . . . didn't have to ask twice.: Erickson, "Cameron Artis-Payne's Long, Winding Road."

91 He wanted to play in the SEC: Erickson, "Cameron Artis-Payne's Long, Winding Road."

91 I was still in shape, and I was ready to play right away.: Erickson, "Cameron Artis-Payne's Long, Winding Road."

92 One night, a car tried . . . the driver was dead.: Erik Brady, "Widow Tells of Bobby Hoppe," *USA Today*, Dec. 23, 2010, http://www.usatoday.com/sports/college/football/2010-12-22.

92 When rumors spread in . . . he confessed to his wife,: Aaron Burns, "An Auburn Football Star, a Killing, and Redemption," *The Auburn Villager*, Oct. 27, 2010, http://www.auburnvillager.com/story.html?1288209317027542.

92 "He suffered so much keeping that terrible secret inside,": Brady, "Widow Tells of Bobby Hoppe."

92 "He told me, 'I'd . . . 'till the day he died.": Burns, "An Auburn Football Star."

92 He finally accepted God's . . . to forgive himself.: Burns, "An Auburn Football Star."

BIBLIOGRAPHY

Anderson, Lars. "Making the Man: Nick Fairley." *Sports Illustrated Presents Auburn Tigers: Pride of the Plains*. New York City: Time, Inc., 2011. 65-67.

---. "Tiger Burning Bright: Cam Newton." *Sports Illustrated Presents Auburn Tigers: Pride of the Plains*. New York City: Time, Inc., 2011. 59-63.

"Auburn Came Back to Subdue a Pair of Touted South Carolina Teams." *The Auburn Villager*. 27 Jan. 2011. 6.

"Auburn Fans Roll Toomer's Corner after Spring Game." *SI.com*. 21 April 2013. http://sportsillustrated.cnn.com/college-football/news/20130421/auburn-toomers-corner.

"Auburn Ranked No. 1 in Latest BCS Rankings." *All In: Auburn's Run to the National Championship*. Cumming, GA: *Ledger-Enquirer*/TD Publishing, 2011. 76-77.

"AU's Championship Warms Housel's Heart." *Montgomery Advertiser*. 10 Sept. 2011. http://psasb.pqarchiver.com/montgomeryadvertiser/access/2451832001.html.

Bettinger, Jim & Julie S. *The Book of Bowden*. Nashville: TowleHousePublishing, 2001.

Bitter, Andy. "Auburn Football: Kodi Burns Settling in at Wide Receiver." *Ledger-Enquirer*. 23 Aug. 2010. http://www.ledger-enquirer.com/2010/08/23/1239684.

---. "Blowout of Louisiana-Monroe. Gives Tigers Fans, Starters a Break." *All In: Auburn's Run to the National Championship*. Cumming, GA: *Ledger-Enquirer*/TD Publishing, 2011. 46-47.

---. "Tigers Keep Finding Ways to Win, Remain Undefeated with Victory over Kentucky." *All In: Auburn's Run to the National Championship*. Cumming, GA: *Ledger-Enquirer*/TD Publishing, 2011. 52-53.

---. "Tigers' New Quarterback Cam Newton Lives Up to Hype." *All In: Auburn's Run to the National Championship*. Cumming, GA: *Ledger-Enquirer*/TD Publishing, 2011. 14-15.

---. "Tigers 'Refuse to Lose.'" *All In: Auburn's Run to the National Championship*. Cumming, GA: *Ledger-Enquirer*/TD Publishing, 2011. 60-61.

---. "Tight End Lutzenkirchen Dances. " *All In: Auburn's Run to the National Championship*. Cumming, GA: *Ledger-Enquirer*/TD Publishing, 2011. 106.

Bolton, Clyde. *War Eagle: A Story of Auburn Football*. Huntsville: The Strode Publishers, 1973.

Brady, Erik. "Widow Tells of Bobby Hoppe, Who Shot Man, Led Auburn to '57 Title." *USA Today*. 23 Dec. 2010. http://www.usatoday.com/sports/college/football/2010-12-22-bobby-hoppe-auburn_N.htm.

Bryant, Bill. "Come-From-Behind Tigers Are Must-See TV." *All in to Win*. Birmingham: *The Birmingham News, Press-Register, The Huntsville Times*, 2011. 85.

---. "Not a Flinch: Resiliency Wins the Day." *All in to Win*. Birmingham: *The Birmingham News, Press-Register, The Huntsville Times*, 2011. 31.

---. "Tigers Are Deeper and More Experienced. Will They Be Better?" *All in to Win*. Birmingham: *The Birmingham News, Press-Register, The Huntsville Times*, 2011. 61.

---. "True Freshman Dyer Is Big Play-Maker." *All in to Win*. Birmingham: *The Birmingham News, Press-Register, The Huntsville Times*, 2011. 28-29.

Burns, Aaron. "An Auburn Football Star, a Killing and Redemption." *The Auburn Villager*. 27 Oct. 2010. http://www.auburnvillager.com/story.html?1288209317027542.

Donnell, Rich. *Shug: The Life and Times of Auburn's Ralph 'Shug' Jordan*. Montgomery: Owl Bay Publishers, 1993.

Erickson, Joel A. "Cameron Artis-Payne's Long, Winding Road to College Football Lands Running Back at Auburn." *al.com*. 18 April 2013. http://www.al.com/auburnfootball/index.ssf/2013/04/cameron_artis-paynes_long_wind.html.

Glier, Ray. *What It Means to Be a Tiger*. Chicago: Triumph Books, 2010.

Goldberg, Charles. "Auburn Beats Ole Miss . . . and the No. 1 Jinx." *All in to Win*. Birmingham: *The Birmingham News, Press-Register, The Birmingham Times*, 2011. 112.

---. "Auburn Defense Does the Job." *All In to Win*. Birmingham: *The*

    Birmingham News, Press-Register, The Huntsville Times, 2011. 16.

---. "Chizik and His Tigers Claim SEC West Title." *All in to Win.* Birmingham: *The Birmingham News, Press-Register, The Huntsville Times,* 2011. 124, 126.

Hemphill, Paul. "Our First Time." *Auburn Magazine.* Fall 2007. 22-31.

Henderson, J. "Genealogy of a Nickname." *The War Eagle Reader.* 11 Sept. 2007. http://thewareaglereader.wordpress.com/2007/09/11.

Hester, Wayne. *Where Tradition Began: The Centennial History of Auburn Football.* Birmingham: Seacoast Publishing/*The Birmingham News,* 1991.

Hicks, Tommy. "Tigers' Patience, Not Speed, Seals BCS Win." *All in to Win.* Birmingham: *The Birmingham News, Press-Register, The Huntsville Times,* 2011. 21.

Higgins, Ron. "A Strange But Fitting Friendship." *SECNation.* 28 Oct. 2010. http://www.secdigitalnetwork.com/SECNation/SECTraditions/tabid/1073/Article/214902.

Hinton, Ed. "Shug's Time to Shine." *Sports Illustrated Presents Auburn Tigers: Pride of the Plains.* New York City: Time, Inc., 2011. 74.

Jenkins, Sally. "Catch This!" *Sports Illustrated.* 24 Oct. 1994. 35-39.

Johnson, Jon. "Former HA Player Watson Downs Performs Well for Auburn." *Dothan Eagle.* 10 Nov. 2010. http://www2.dothaneagle.com/sports/2010/nov/10.

Kausler, Don, Jr. "Come-From-Behind Slugfest Puts Tide Under." *All in to Win.* Birmingham: *The Birmingham News, Press-Register, The Huntsville Times,* 2011. 130.

Kay, Julie. "Leap of Faith: Olympic Diver Garcia Finds His Beliefs a Help in Sports World." *The Advocate.* 14 Aug. 2004. http://us.mg2.mail.yahoo.com/dc/launch?gx=1&.rand=62u6vmak9i5ru.

Kennedy, Randy. "Newton Lives Up to the Hype." *All in to Win.* Birmingham: *The Birmingham News, Press-Register, the Huntsville Times,* 2011. 67.

Low, Chris. "Josh Bynes Has Been Auburn's Rock." *College Football Nation Blog.* 8 Jan. 2011. http://espn.go.com/blog/ncfnation/post/_/id/37694.

Maisel, Ivan and Kelly Whiteside. *A War in Dixie.* New York City: HarperCollins Publishers, 2001.

Mandel, Stewart. "Race to the End Zone." *Sports Illustrated Presents Auburn Tigers: Pride of the Plains.* New York City: Time, Inc., 2011. 27.

Marshall, Phillip. *The Auburn Experience: The Traditions and Heroes of Auburn Athletics.* Auburn: Phillip Marshall, 2004.

McCarter, Mark. "Auburn's 1957 National Championship Came From Nowhere." *The Huntsville Times.* 6 Jan. 2011. http://www.al.com/sports/index.ssf/2011/01/auburn_1957_national_champions.html.

---. "Auburn's Quindarius Carr Nearing End of 'Blessed' Career as Tigers' Receiver." *The Huntsville Times.* 25 Nov. 2011. http://www.al.com/sports/index.ssf.2011/11.

---. "The Comeback." *All in to Win.* Birmingham: *The Birmingham News, Press-Register, The Huntsville Times,* 2011. 133.

Moon, Josh. "Tigers Saved by Bell in Key Moments: Young Auburn DB Makes Big Plays." *Montgomery Advertiser.* 30 Nov. 2010. https://secure.pqarchiver.com/montgomeryadvertiser/access/2200659421.

---. "Turning Point: Zachery's TD Early in 3rd Quarter Gave Auburn Hope." *Montgomery Advertiser.* 27 Nov. 2010. https://secure.pqarchiver.com/montgomeryadvertiser/access/2198638751.

---. "Ziemba's Superstitions Take the Cake." *Montgomery Advertiser.* 9 Jan. 2011. https://secure.pqarchiver.com/montgomeryadvertiser/access/2233186191.

Murphy, Austin. "Iron Giants." *Sports Illustrated Presents Auburn Tigers: Pride of the Plains.* New York City: Time, Inc., 2011. 35-36.

---. "On the Biggest Stage, New Stars Emerged." *Sports Illustrated Presents Auburn Tigers: Pride of the Plains.* New York City: Time, Inc., 2011. 42-52.

Murphy, Mark. *Game of My Life: Auburn: Memorable Stories of Tigers Football.* Champaign IL: Sports Publishing L.L.C., 2007.

Oliver, Kristen. "'New' Toomer's Corner Will Blend Past and Present Traditions." *oanow.*

com. 20 April 2013. http://www.oanow.com/news/toomers_oaks/article.

Plexico, Van Allen and John Ringer. *Season of Our Dreams: The 2010 Auburn Tigers*. White Rocket Books, 2011.

Schroeder, George. "The Visionary: Gus Malzahn." *Sports Illustrated Presents Auburn Tigers: Pride of the Plains*. New York City: Time, Inc., 2011. 69-71.

Scott, Richard. *An Inside Look at a Perfect Season: Tales from the Auburn 2004 Championship Season*. Champaign, IL: Sports Publishing L.L.C., 2005.

Smothers, Jimmy. "Gross Recalls Being Part of Auburn's '57 Title Team." *Gadsden Times*. 9 Jan. 2011. http://www.gadsdentimes.com/article/20110109/news/110109839?p=4&tc=pg.

Solomon, Jon. "Can They Keep the Big Mo?" *All in to Win*. Birmingham: *The Birmingham News, Press-Register, The Huntsville Times*, 2011. 90-91.

---. "Chizik to Offense: Get It Together." *All in to Win*. Birmingham: *The Birmingham News, Press-Register, The Huntsville Times*, 2011. 78-79.

---. "Finally in the Big Show." *All in to Win*. Birmingham: *The Birmingham News, Press-Register, The Huntsville Times*, 2011. 44.

Staples, Andy. "A Defense to Lean On." *Sports Illustrated Presents Auburn Tigers: Pride of the Plains*. New York City: Time, Inc., 2011. 15.

---. "Up in the Air." *Sports Illustrated Presents Auburn Tigers: Pride of the Plains*. New York City: Time, Inc., 2011. 39.

"Steve Gandy." *The Sports Xchange*. 10 Feb. 2012. http://www.nfldraftscout.com/ratings/dsprofile.php?pyid=16976&draftyear=2009.

Szvetitz, Mike. "Final Roll Celebrates Toomer's Corner Past, Present and Future." *oanow.com*. 20 April 2013. http://www.oanow.com/news/toomers_oaks/article.

Tankersley, Mike. "Auburn's Trench Stars Bask in Title." *Montgomery Advertiser*. 9 Feb. 2011. https://secure.pqarchiver.com/montgomeryadvertiser/access/2272893491.html.

Tate, Jay G. "(23) Auburn 42, Utah State 38 -- AU-spicious Start: Tigers Avoid Upset Bid." *Montgomery Advertiser*. 4 Sept. 2011. https://secure.pqarchiver.com/montgomeryadvertiser/access/2442449391.html.

---. "Auburn Atlanta Bound." *All In: Auburn's Incredible Run to the National Championship*. Chicago: Triumph Books/ *Montgomery Advertiser*, 2011. 99, 101.

---. "Auburn Football: Ziemba's Speech Credited in AU's Drive Toward Win." *Montgomery Advertiser*. 13 Oct. 2010. https://secure.pqarchiver.com/montgomeryadvertiser/access/2161377811.

---. "Auburn Notebook: Backup Jessel Curry Taking Notes Watching Josh Bynes Play." *Montgomery Advertiser*. 23 Sept. 2010. https://secure.pqarchiver.com/montgomeryadvertiser/access/2144737031.

---. "Auburn's Burns Enjoys Life on the Other Side of Passes." *Montgomery Advertiser*. 17 Aug. 2010. https://secure.pqarchiver.com/montgomeryadvertiser/access/2118297881.

---. "Auburn's Mosley Makes Best of Opportunity." *Montgomery Advertiser*. 13 Sept. 2010. https://secure.pqarchiver.com/montgomeryadvertiser/access/2136528671.

---. "Auburn's Sullen Gets Svelte." *Montgomery Advertiser*. 7 Aug. 2010. https://secure.pqarchiver.com/montgomeryadvertiser/access/2103123821.

---. "AU's Washington Makes an Impact on Special Teams." *Montgomery Advertiser*. 5 Nov. 2010. https://secure.pqarchiver.com/montgomeryadvertiser/access/2180801301.

---. "Comeback Tigers Do It Again." *All In: Auburn's Incredible Run to the National Championship*. Chicago: Triumph Books/ *Montgomery Advertiser*, 2011. 57, 59.

---. "Iron Bowl: Burns' Unselfishness Seen as a Catalyst in AU's Resurgence." *Montgomery Advertiser*. 23 Nov. 2010. https://secure.pqarchiver.com/montgomeryadvertiser/access/2195168321.

---. "Lutzenkirchen's Patience Paying Off with New Role." *Montgomery Advertiser*. 30 Sept. 2010. https://secure.pqarchiver.com/montgomeryadvertiser/access/2150514211.

MORE AUBURN

---. "New Auburn QB Newton Lays Down Law, Makes Huge First Impression." *All In: Auburn's Incredible Run to the National Championship*. Chicago: Triumph Books/ *Montgomery Advertiser*, 2011. 37-38.

---. "Newton's Law: Auburn on Brink of Greatness." *Montgomery Advertiser*. 28 Aug. 2010. https://secure.pqarchiver.com/montgomeryadvertiser/access/2124632701.

---. "No Pain, No Gain: LB Bynes Earns Tigers' Trust on Defense with His Durability." *Montgomery Advertiser*. 23 Sept. 2010. https://secure.pqarchiver.com/montgomery advertiser/access/2144737041.

---. "Pile-Moving Play in LSU Contest Indicative of Improvements from Auburn's Offensive Line, Run Game." *Montgomery Advertiser*. 28 Oct. 2010. https://secure.pqarchiver. com/montgomeryadvertiser/access/2174413861.

---. "Tigers Trump 'Trap Game.'" *All In: Auburn's Incredible Run to the National Championship*. Chicago: Triumph Books/ *Montgomery Advert.ser*, 2011. 89, 91.

---. "'We Refuse to Lose.'" *All In: Auburn's Incredible Run to the National Championship*. Chicago: Triumph Books/*Montgomery Advertiser*, 2011. 73, 75.

Thomas, Landon. *The SEC Team of the '80s: Auburn Football 1980-89*. Woodstock, GA: Tiger Publishing, 2004.

White, Chris. "Wide Receiver Darvin Adams Sets SEC Championship Game Record." *All In: Auburn's Incredible Run to the National Championship*. Chicago: Triumph Books/ *Montgomery Advertiser*, 2011. 124-25.

Williams, Chette. *Hard Fighting Soldier*. Decatur, GA: Looking Glass Books, Inc., 2007.

Woodbery, Evan. "4th Quarter Turnovers Put Tigers on Top." *All In to Win*. Birmingham: *The Birmingham News, Press-Register, The Huntsville Times*, 2011. 82, 85.

---. "A Heart-Stopping Win." *All In to Win*. Birmingham: *The Birmingham News, Press-Register, The Huntsville Times*, 2011. 76.

---. "A Win with Style." *All In to Win*. Birmingham: *The Birmingham News, Press-Register, The Huntsville Times*, 2011. 88.

---. "Auburn Linebacker Josh Bynes Doesn't Let Lack of Shoes Interrupt Media Days Appearance." *al.com*. 23 July 2010. http://www.al.com/sports/index.ssf/2010/07/ josh_bynes_blog_entry.html.

---. "Auburn's Chances Up in the Air." *All In to Win*. Birmingham: *The Birmingham News, Press-Register, The Huntsville Times*, 2011. 60.

---. "Auburn's Special Teams Help Seal Chick-Fil-A Bowl Win." *al.com*. 31 Dec. 2011. http:// www.al.com/sports/index.ssf/2011/12.

---. "Defense Dominates: Tigers Grab Narrow Victory." *All In to Win*. Birmingham: *The Birmingham News, Press-Register, The Huntsville Times*, 2011. 70-71.

---. "Grading the Tigers." *All in to Win*. Birmingham: *The Birmingham News, Press-Register, The Huntsville Times*, 2011. 19.

---. "Rematch in Atlanta Gives Tigers SEC Championship." *All In to Win*. Birmingham: *The Birmingham News, Press-Register, The Huntsville Times*, 2011. 40, 42.

---. "Wildcats on the Run." *All In to Win*. Birmingham: *The Birmingham News, Press-Register, The Huntsville Times*, 2011. 94, 96.

Zenor, John. "Auburn's Towel-Waving Trooper Taylor Keeps Things Loose." *GoVolsXtra*. 9 Jan. 2011. http://www.govolsxtra.com/news/2011/jan/09.

Zimanek, Brad. "Montgomery Family Enjoying Auburn's Tide to National Title Game." *Montgomery Advertiser*. 5 Jan. 2011. https://secure.pqarchiver.com/montgomery advertiser/access/2229892471.

TIGERS

INDEX
(LAST NAME, DEVOTION DAY NUMBER)

203

MORE AUBURN